Other Titles in the Capital Savvy Series:

SAVVY INTERVIEWING

How to Ace the Interview & Get the Job

John Van Devender
Gloria Van Devender-Graves

Capital Savvy Series

CAPITAL
BOOKS, INC.
Sterling, Virginia

Capital Books, Inc.
P.O. Box 605
Herndon, Virginia 20172-0605

ISBN 10: 1-933102-32-2 (alk. paper)
ISBN 13: 978-1-933102-32-0

Library of Congress Cataloging-in-Publication Data

Van Devender, John.
    Savvy interviewing: how to ace the interview & get the job / John Van Devender, Gloria Van Devender-Graves. – 1st ed.
        p. cm. – (Capital savvy series)
    Includes index.
    ISBN-13: 978-1-933102-32-0 (alk. paper)
    ISBN-10: 1-933102-32-2
    1. Employment interviewing. I Van Devender-Graves, Gloria. II. Title. III. Series.

    HF5549.5.I6V36 2006
    650. 14'4–dc22

                                            2006033148

Printed in the United States of America on acid-free paper that meets the American National Standards Institute Z39-48 Standard.

First Edition

10 9 8 7 6 5 4 3 2 1

Dedication

To those undecorated, unsung foot soldiers who
make everything work—professional
Human Resources Managers

"Employ experienced people. But before you act on
anyone's word, go and see for yourself."
—Ambrosius Aurelius, Count of Britain, mid-fifth century

THEN

"Regardless of size, regardless of location, regardless of affiliation with any special organization, every business has an opportunity—and an obligation—to do what business does best. And that is to hire people, train them, and place them in productive jobs."

—John D. Harper, President and CEO, Alcoa, speech to the Economic Club of Detroit, Feb. 24, 1969

NOW

"I don't find loyalty to be a great corporate value. What good did a guarantee of lifetime employment do for the employees of IBM when everyone was buying Dell and HP computers? Only winning companies count. Winning is good. Winning companies and the people who work for them make the country go. That's my definition of social responsibility."

—Jack Welch, CEO of General Electric (retired), business forum, University of Chicago, June 1, 2005

CONTENTS

A FAIRY TALE FOR OUR TIME

It's a dangerous business going out your front door.
J. R. R. Tolkien

Once upon a time not long ago, employers wanted to give you a job, no questions asked, or almost. Employees were treated with dignity and respect. Compensation was fair, benefits and vacations were generous, and management wanted everyone to be satisfied with their work.

Corporations operated by consensus and moved slowly, like brontosaurs. For the most part, they were careful not to break things. Life at all job levels was serene, predictable, and dull. Initiative was not encouraged, except within carefully pre-scribed limits, because an excitable brontosaur might forget to watch where it was putting its big feet. Companies shared their profits with employees and shareholders and spread the rest around their communities in the form of donations to the per-forming arts, hospitals, or colleges. If you came to work on time and didn't commit a felony, the odds were pretty good that after thirty years of putting your feet under the same table, you could count on retiring with a pension, medical benefits, and a little something extra socked away in the company savings plan.

Alas, like dinosaurs that were erased by a giant meteorite millions of years ago, the paternalistic companies whose mission was to create a job for every American who wanted to work vanished along with leisure suits, 8-track tapes, Betamax, and *The Love Boat*. In the space of a few short years, many respected and well-known corporate brands disappeared under a relentless tide of hostile takeovers.

The takeover artists and the banks that financed the breaking up of corporate America made enormous amounts of money buying companies and selling off the pieces. This national buying and selling frenzy created no additional value; no more than Daylight Saving Time adds more hours to a day. These deals were financed through synergies, which is business-speak for consolidating functions and laying off thousands of workers.

Managers whose pay and perks suddenly exceeded the gross national product of some small countries justified these actions by talking about improving shareholder value, but they were preaching to an empty church because shareholders in the form of ordinary Americans no longer called the shots, unless you counted a few East Coast brokerage firms and multi-national banks. Managers desperate to pay off the huge debt incurred by the takeovers became slavishly focused on currying favor with Wall Street where the six or ten financial analysts who followed their particular industry eagerly waited to whack them for missing quarterly earnings forecasts.

Out of this bubbling cauldron the present "value-added" business world was born. Improving the bottom line is now an all-consuming passion, religious in intensity. It's a brave new world of pressure, re-education, long hours, and insecurity, where loyalty is extended not to your entire organization, but mainly to your business unit, your work team, or to anyone who can help you rise. It's a world in flux, with unclear boundaries and shifting rules. In other words, it's a chaotic, uncertain job market.

Life at the top is no longer a stroll in the park for today's executives. Managers today are smarter and tougher and better educated than their predecessors, and they have to be to keep both eyes on the ball because when they are home asleep at night, their competitors on the other side of the world are wide awake and plotting mischief. Executive shakeups are regular occurrences, like snowstorms in Alaska, only more often. And these shakeups affect everybody in the food chain.

What does this modern fairy tale mean to you, the anxious jobseeker? Simply this:

> Where there is chaos, there is also opportunity. And knowing how companies operate and what they want from you can be a great advantage.

There are plenty of wonderful jobs out there waiting for somebody just like you to grab them by the throat and knock their socks off. If you embrace this new reality and share the urgency, passion, and commitment, you will be welcomed as a valued contributor to the team and compensated accordingly.

If you survive your interview, that is!

CHAPTER 1

OKAY, YOU GOT THE INTERVIEW! NOW WHAT?

For many are called, but few are chosen.

—Matthew 22:14

Congratulations! You did something right to get this far, through networking, a recruiter, an advertisement, a friend, the Internet, or blind dumb luck.

Or perhaps you're still waiting to hear from your employer of choice to grant you an interview. No matter.

The point is, within two or three minutes after you meet a hiring manager or a Human Resources (HR) recruiter, these people will make a snap judgment about you and your abilities.

And that judgment will be either to continue to treat you as a serious candidate until you stumble, or to dismiss your chances altogether and simply go through the motions of an interview to meet legal and corporate policy requirements.

It's to your advantage to keep us interested in you as long as possible, or at least until we see everything that you have under the hood. This little book will help you turn the tide. It contains a lot of secrets about interviewing that every job candidate ought to know—and that nobody will tell you. We—the authors,

Human Resource experts—have interviewed and made hiring recommendations on hundreds of people, so we know our stuff. Read, learn, and take heart. It may be a jungle out there, but you don't have to walk through it alone.

What's Here, and What's Not

We aren't going to advise you about the networking part of your job search, which is a long, tough, and complicated process all by itself. Besides, a thriving industry already exists to help you do that. We're going to help you do what those outfits can't do for you, and that's to help you survive your interview. The networking experts, as good as they are, haven't a clue about that. How could they? They don't actually hire anyone. That's not their job. It's our job.

The best way to start is to let you in on a few of the secrets that can stop you dead in your tracks. Because guess what?

Most often, it's not the wrong answer to a question that will spike your chances.

Besides, if you are a quality applicant, you will have the right answers. So here's a news flash for you: It's not generally what you say to our questions that will help us to decide whether to give you a nice seat in our corporate coliseum or toss you back with the lions. It's everything else about you. Chiefly, we're interested in your appearance, how you handle yourself under fire, and what's on your resume.

One more thing. The authors have worked for large and small companies and the rules for interviewing are the same. The only real difference between a large business and a small one is how the workload is distributed. You can stay in the same niche throughout your entire career in a giant corporation or a huge government bureaucracy. In a medium-sized or small company, the division of labor is much less formal. In these companies, employees are expected to lend a hand wherever it is needed. Suppose, for example, you have applied for a position as an accountant. In a large corporation, you may be interviewed by two Human Resources managers, the vice-president of finance, the hiring manager, and your group or department supervisor. In a small company the same person may perform all of those functions. But large company or small, the bottom-line question we have for you is identical: What can you do to help make us a winner?

CHAPTER 2

FIRST THINGS FIRST: YOUR RESUME

I have tried simply to write the best I can. Sometimes I have good luck and write better than I can.

—Ernest Hemingway

Wait just a minute!

Why is a book about surviving an interview wasting your time by discussing your resume? Aren't there a thousand people who can prepare a professional resume for you? Yes. Maybe ten thousand. And if the folks who you paid to do these things for you actually did them correctly, we wouldn't need to talk about this.

Take a look at this list of "do nots." Then run through your resume again, one final time, to see if you have accidentally hit any of these potential job-killing speed bumps.

Here's the list:

- **Do not** ever put your social security number on your resume, or on any document containing your address. Identity theft is a huge and growing problem. Most resumes circulate on the Internet, and everything that was ever placed on the Internet is still out there somewhere in cyberspace. Giving us your social security number tells us you're clueless about life in the twenty-first century. Not a good start!

- **Do not** reveal your marital status, the state of your health, or information about your children. We don't want to know anything about you that isn't strictly professional.
- **Do not** include your photo.
- **Do not** send us DVDs, CD-ROMs, videos, audiotapes, newspaper clippings, or portfolios unless we specifically ask you for them. We're not going to return anything to you. We get hundreds of resumes a day, and although we may retain them for affirmative action or company policy requirements, all unsolicited supporting material goes straight to the dumpster.
- **Do not** include information about your website unless you are a web designer, e-commerce technician, or an intranet content manager. Be warned: Topless photos of your spouse or girlfriend on your site will not advance your cause. Or the photo of you pouring beer on your head. Purge your site before you ask us to look at it. Some companies may "google" you before the interview. Be professional!
- **Do not** use sidebars, boxes, rules, columns, cute graphics, photos, colored ink, shading, animation, artsy-type fonts, or weird punctuation on your resume. Use a plain font like Helvetica, Courier, Ariel, or Times New Roman that has stood the test of time.
- **Do not** use colored paper. But why are you sending out paper resumes at all? This is a technical age. You should be e-mailing or faxing your resume, or applying via our company website. Some experienced job seekers won't even apply to companies that ask for paper resumes. Take it from us: You want a career with a company that has good internal information technology. Companies without good communications

technology aren't going to be around long enough for you to have any sort of career. See Chapter 3 for tips on submitting electronic resumes. **Do not** use more than two resume pages, and **do not** use very small type to stuff your entire life history on those two pages. If you can't condense your vital information, or if you can't write, it's okay to pay somebody to do it for you.

- **Do not** tell us about every job you had since you were in high school, unless you are just entering the workforce. If you have a lot of experience, all we want to know about is what you did during the past ten years.

Now here are the **Do's**:

- **Do** use "Key Words." Nobody shuffles through stacks of resumes anymore. If you have applied directly to a company or through an Internet job search provider, your resume will be stored in a data warehouse for a certain period of time where corporate recruiters or hiring managers may access it by looking for key words. Key words are a kind of shortcut code for whatever the hiring manager requires in an applicant. Key words are usually technical: "Oracle database manager" or "Microsoft Project skills." They may also include special character traits such as a "sense of humor," or professional certifications such as "Certified Public Accountant (CPA)."
- Never write: "I am an expert at Microsoft Office." Be specific: "I am an expert at PowerPoint, Project, Excel, and PageMaker." (And in today's highly competitive job market, you had better be an expert in Microsoft Office. It's an electronic world. If you can't run a spreadsheet,

prepare a simple slide presentation, or outline a project, consider taking a class or asking a friend to teach you before you start your job search. And if you have mastered a graphics software package and bring us samples, we're going to be very impressed with you.)

Your resume probably won't be seen without the right key words. Try to anticipate what the hiring manager *really* wants. Remember our little fairy tale? Use key words to describe how your skills and experience will add value to the bottom line. As nerdy as it may sound, everything on your resume should be aimed like a *Star Trek* photon torpedo at telling us why YOU are the right person for the job.

- **Do** provide plenty of contact information. People have active lives, and we are a mobile society. Make it easy for us to reach you. Just like you, we sometimes work through lunch and into the evening, and occasionally on weekends. (You do that also, don't you? Because if you don't, you're not going to last very long in today's business world). List your day phone, night phone, cell phone, and e-mail address. Make sure you have an answering machine because we may call and e-mail you simultaneously.

- **Do** police your voicemail. The voice on your answering machine will very likely be our first impression of you. Avoid humor: "This is John's bookie, and he can't come to the phone right now." Avoid religious themes. You may have a truly blessed life but unless you are applying for a ministerial post, please leave preaching to the professionals. Never allow your children to record "cute" messages. Barking dogs are *never* cute; they are annoying. These are all extremely *major* offenses. If you are guilty as charged, change your voicemail *RIGHT NOW!* (After you get hired, you can change it back.)

- **Do** make sure your e-mail address is professional. Internet names like Goodtimegirl or Drunknhappy are not amusing. They are frivolous, gross, and inappropriate. An Internet name like Giggles will not win you an interview for that executive secretary position in a prestigious law office, although a trendy advertising agency looking for a bubbly traffic manager or an outgoing receptionist may welcome you with open arms. If you have properly researched our company (you *did* research our company, didn't you?), you will understand how and where the job you applied for fits into our corporate environment.

- **Do** print out your resume and review it. Hand it to some friends and ask them to review it. Listen to them if they suggest changes. If you don't listen to people who know you and want you to succeed, what chance do you think you'll have with us? Does your information make sense? If you can't manage to put together a complete thought, you're not going to work here. We notice those things.

- **Do** provide references or salary requirements if we ask for them.

- **Do** follow the directions on the job advertisement. Did you read it all the way to the end? Good for you. Now read it again. Before you send us your resume, be sure you followed the directions *exactly*.

- **Do** check your spelling. Even one little mistake can disqualify you. It's not unfair; it's how we separate the wheat from the chaff. Quality is a big deal in today's business world. Participate. Show us you care.

What about a Cover Letter?

Well, it depends.

Some recruiters prefer them. Others will skip cover letters and go right to your resume. It can't hurt to include one, but before you send it, **Do** review the last two **Do's**. If we find an error in your cover letter, you won't be coming to see us.

Some Advice on Internet Job Sites

There are a lot of bad neighborhoods on the Internet. Job-hunting websites to help you with your career search come and go. Next to the blue screen of death when the hard drive fails on your PC, there's nothing more annoying than seeing the message: "404 Not Found" when you're surfing the web looking for a non-existent URL. And that's not the only problem. Many Internet sites have been abandoned, and the content is hopelessly out of date. Still others contain gross inaccuracies or just plain wrong information, especially regarding salary information (but we'll get to salaries in Chapters 10 and 16). Remember, anyone can start a website on any subject! That said, Careerbuilder.com, Monster.com, and Salary.com have been around for some time and contain generally reliable data. Monster.com also has a useful section on salaries.

CHAPTER 3

I CAN'T HEAR YOUR PC

It weighs 200 pounds, but if you want it portable, we'll make it portable. We'll put a handle on it.
—electronics company engineer

We've been talking about computers and communication technology, as you've probably noticed. That's one big reason it's called the Information Age. We have a lot more to say about this topic so hang in there.

You say your PC at home is brand new, with the latest operating system and the newest software updates? Hooray for you, but guess what?

Your PC may be overqualified for your job search. Older computers can't hear what your machine is trying to tell them unless you dumb it down some.

(And because upgrading hundreds of PCs is outrageously expensive, most of us in the workplace have older computers.)

Most very large company database job search systems—and virtually all government agencies—cannot use files directly from your PC. (Most government agencies cannot even swap files with each other.)

For starters, our software may be older than Julius Caesar. Or the blacksmith may simply have quit making parts for our hardware. And for small companies there is the ever-present threat of viruses (big companies have platoons of IT [Information Technology] professionals and firewalls to detect and disinfect viruses before they do damage). These are just some of the reasons why many employers will ask you to either re-key certain portions of your resume, or to paste parts of your resume into a word processing format their computers can understand.

That is why almost nobody will accept your resume as an attachment to a cover letter. If you are actually asked to forward a resume, dumb it down. Send it as a rich text format file (rtf), or as a Word 95 6.0 document (or both). Whether you are sending your resume to a high-speed laptop in an upscale Madison Avenue PR agency or to a cranky, museum-eligible PC in a sheepherder's hut in Outer Mongolia, both machines will be able to read either format.

Did You Connect *All* the Dots?

Yes, re-keying and/or cutting and pasting are boring. Yes, truncating your beautiful and lovingly handcrafted resume is tragic and can take up to an hour on some job sites. Do it anyway. Do whatever we tell you to do—exactly.

CHAPTER 4

ABOUT US, YOUR FRIENDLY CORPORATE RECRUITER

A team should be an extension of a coach's personality. My teams are arrogant and obnoxious.

—Al McGuire

Human Resources managers are jerks, sometimes.

It's what we're paid for. We're the professional gatekeepers. We like our companies a lot, and you aren't coming to work here unless we like you. Besides, nearly everybody at our company hates us. The only time we interact with other employees is to warn them about some petty policy infraction, or to tell them the company is reducing one of their benefits, or that they're being laid off or fired. Our chief executive is convinced that the Human Resources function costs too much money and that there are too many of us for the limited value we provide.

We're a lot like lawyers—a necessary evil. Our jobs are not easy. So don't give us a hard time.

Specifically . . .

If our ad says no phone calls, we mean it. Don't call us. Don't e-mail. Don't walk in and ask for an interview. It's presumptuous, and besides, we don't have time for you.

Don't call to ask us if we got your resume. It's annoying, and it says something uncomplimentary about you that you feel you are more important than everyone else that applied for one of our jobs. Companies are required to send you a card acknowledging the receipt of your resume. In practice, not everybody complies with this, especially in small, less competitive markets. You will probably be notified, but the world is full of uncertainty. There are no guarantees.

We really hate tire kickers; so don't apply for multiple jobs on our website. Send us *one* resume for the job you really want.

Corporate Recruiters vs. Staffing Agents: What's the Difference?

Corporate recruiters work in the Human Resources department and recruiting is just one of many HR specialties. Other HR functions include training, benefits, pension administration, payroll, employee communications, labor relations, and managing compliance with federal and state employment laws.

Staffing agencies are not part of our company; they are part of a huge industry that covers a wide range of jobs from industrial production workers to chief executive officers of Fortune 500 firms. There is a staffing agency specializing in every job niche you can imagine and for hundreds of positions you've never even heard of.

A lot of temporary administrative and production workers are hired through staffing agencies because these jobs share so many common characteristics that it's easy to find people to fill them. Most workers who fill temp jobs are not highly skilled. In effect, they are interchangeable human parts. But after they prove themselves, many temp workers wind up getting permanent job offers from their new company. Some have even ascended into the rarified air of upper management. But the point is, low-level or high-level, staffing agents play in a totally different ballpark than corporate recruiters.

Staffing agents are sales people who work on commission. Staffing agents might have picked your resume off the Internet (unless you sent it directly to them), or a company might have contracted with them to fill a specialized position. They don't get paid until they place you. Their fee is a big percentage of your first year's salary, paid by us, your new company. Staffing agents add tens of thousands of dollars to the hiring process.

Most staffing agents are competent professionals. But there are a few bad apples in every barrel, and some agents will say anything to their clients or to a candidate to make a sale. Competent or not, their goal is to fill open slots with warm bodies. They work very hard at this because they have to find the right candidates and sell them to us. The problem here for you is they can't tell you how to interview with us. They may tell you they know our culture, but unless they work with our company on a regular basis (and few do), they won't know us well enough to give you good advice.

Staffing agencies use tests to screen people. Oftentimes, they use a lot of tests. Be prepared to jump through hoops. But even if they select you, you will still have to interview with an HR recruiter and the hiring manager. We might not want to work with a staffing agent because we have to pay his fee, or because he screwed us in the past with a bad candidate, even though that's not your fault. But in fairness, maybe that's the only way you can get hired at a firm that has outsourced its hiring function. In that case, they might not accept you as a candidate unless you deal with a staffing agent.

Once you start working with a staffing agency, you're stuck with them throughout the hiring process.

You can't drop them and try to work directly with the hiring company because neither the agent nor the company wants to void a contract and invite a lawsuit. Some agents charge candidates a direct fee for their services, but why would you want to pay someone when you can apply to us yourself for free? It usually makes good sense to research your industry, pick the firms you want to work for, and apply directly to them. But it never hurts to send resumes to staffing agents who specialize in placing people with your skills. Who knows? You might get lucky.

CHAPTER 5

TYPES OF INTERVIEWS

The best feeling in the world is when everyone says you can't do something, and then you do it.
　　　　　　　　—Joey Porter, linebacker, Pittsburgh Steelers

Interviews are a lot like people; they come in all sizes and shapes. There are group interviews, lunch interviews, behavioral interviews, and competency interviews, just to list a few. There are many others, and each has its variations; and then there are interview styles and techniques. It's actually pretty scary stuff, and frankly, there's such a thing as having too much information. So we've decided all you really need to know is the barest of bare bones.

What you also need to know is that each of your encounters with a hiring manager will be a unique learning experience, because every hiring manager is an individual, no matter what interview technique he or she may use. And of course, some hiring managers don't have what you'd call a recognizable interview technique, so if they appear to be just winging it, maybe they are, because that's what works best for them.

Either that, or they may just be really lousy interviewers.

Here's a handy list of interview types and how to handle them. Be aware that you will rarely encounter interviews in a pure form like this. What you are far more likely to see are various pieces of different interviews all mixed together like the mystery casseroles your mother used to make with leftovers.

Practice the action steps listed in each summary! Remember, football players don't show up just on game day. They practice all the time, for as long as it takes. Actors don't wait until they are in front of the camera to look at their scripts. Neither should you. Dress up in your interview clothes, sit in front of a mirror and rehearse, or role-play with a friend. And stay frosty. In an interview, there are no hard and fast right or wrong answers. If you don't handle yourself like a pro the first time out of the box, so what? You have only to watch any major league baseball or football game to realize that highly compensated professionals have their good days and their bad days, just like the rest of us.

Telephone Screen Interview

Used by companies and recruiters to eliminate candidates who are unqualified or who fall outside the salary range. For more detailed information, see Chapters 6 and 7.

Your Goal: Get to the next level.

Your Action: Have your notes ready. Be professional. Stand up! Project energy so your enthusiasm comes across at the other end of the telephone. Answer each question clearly, briefly, and then shut up. When you get invited for a face-to-face interview, then you can dazzle the interviewer with all your qualifications, skills, and specific examples.

One-on-One Interview

Most common interview type. May be informal, highly structured formal, or unstructured formal.

Informal one-on-one interviews are the best and worst of interviews. If an interviewer knows what she's doing, she can learn a great deal about you and your qualifications in a few minutes. If she isn't organized, the interview becomes a pleasant conversation about a special interest like movies or sports. In these cases, you might have enjoyed yourself, but you haven't been interviewed, and the skills you might bring to this job are still a mystery to the company.

Your Goal: It depends. How are things going?

Your Action: If the interviewer is doing a great job bringing your qualifications for the job out into the open, even if she is co-mingling interview questions along with personal commentary about mutual interests or hobbies, you need do nothing except go with the flow. Answer her questions and provide examples as needed to back up your statements. If the interviewer appears disorganized or goes off on a tangent, you will have to take a more proactive role to get back on track. Check out "unstructured one-on-one formal interviews," also under this heading, for a suggestion on managing your way through this situation.

A highly structured one-on-one formal interview is a dance where the other person always leads. Every candidate gets asked the same questions based on the position requirements. An evaluation is made based on notes or, in extreme cases, a numerical grade.

Your Goal: Put your best foot forward.

Your Action: Reply briefly and bring up any qualifications or examples that make you the best candidate.

An unstructured one-on-one formal interview can be quite enjoyable or a recipe for disaster. The interviewer may ask you a few job-related questions and go off on a tangent. An urgent telephone call or business interruption may derail his train of thought. He might simply have misplaced your resume and the job description. He might be filling in for someone else. Or he might be a really bad interviewer. If things start to slide out of reach, don't panic. Just be prepared to take over.

Your Goal: Get back on track.

Your Action: Politely redirect the flow of conversation back to the task at hand. Sample response: "I'm really enjoying our conversation, and I appreciate your taking the time to put me at ease, especially when I know how busy you must be. Can you tell me what your personal expectations are for this position?

Sequential Interview

Your interview may last an hour or run all day long, but you will meet with only one person at a time. One of the interviewers will be your supervisor. You may also be interviewed by your supervisor's boss, your co-workers, and relevant department heads. Any of these interviews can torpedo you. Treat each meeting as a separate, make-or-break interview, because that's what it is. They might all ask you the same questions. Most likely, you will experience many highly unusual and interesting interview styles, since so few people are properly trained in interview techniques.

Your Goal: Survive and prevail. Find a way to make them remember you.

Your Action: Be prepared to be asked and to answer the same questions all day long. While you're doing that, look for a way to differentiate yourself from every other candidate they have interviewed. Suggested response: "I can't help noticing you have a Jack Vance novel on your shelf. He's one of my favorite fantasy authors." (If the interviewer shows any interest, you can follow up with your shopping trip to a used bookstore in a bad neighborhood where you purchased a dozen of Vance's out-of-print books; or talk about the fan letter you wrote him and how he actually replied). Okay, it's an extreme example. But it's an extremely competitive job market. If you don't pounce on every opportunity that comes your way, shame on you.

Group Interview

These are conducted by some of the people you will interact with in your new job. They may be part of your work team, in which case they'll be closely watching everything you do and say. They may or may not have a list of prepared questions. This is a very tough and extremely stressful interview situation. (For an example of a group interview, see Chapter 6, "We're Arrogant, and We're Ganging Up on You.")

Your Goal: Impress them.

Your Action: Forget about scoring any points early in this game. Play defense, until you know how things stand. Even if they introduce themselves, if it's a large crowd, you won't know who they all are or what they do. Treat each person as if she's your new boss. Focus completely on whomever has just asked you a question. Respond directly to that person. When you have finished speaking, make eye contact with everyone in the room until someone asks the next question.

Panel Interview

This is a highly structured small group interview. One person asks all the questions, another takes notes, and a third person observes your body language. Treat this exactly like a structured one-on-one interview.

Competency Interview

A relatively recent development at a growing number of large and medium-sized firms is interviewing for competencies. This method replaces or augments more traditional methods of interviewing for the technical skills highlighted in your resume. If you have ever had a competency interview, you will find it very different than the normal run of interviews. In addition to the technical requirements of the job, the company will have assigned various competencies to the job description. Competencies are an attempt to predict how you will succeed by assessing the attitudes and behaviors you bring to your new job.

There are dozens of different competencies. Every job at a firm practicing competency hiring will have assigned to it as many as six competencies. Competencies for a sales position, for example, might include ethics and values, sizing up people, negotiating, technical learning, and problem-solving, just to name a few.[1]

If you were interviewing for the position of executive assistant for three senior managers of the firm, the competencies for this job might include setting priorities, comfort around top management, integrity and trust, listening, and organizational ability.[2] These would be in addition to the technical skills called for in the job description.

Questions in a competency interview are open-ended: "Tell me about the time . . ." sorts of questions designed to promote dialogue and probe into how you handled some past event—how you felt, what you said, and what resulted from your actions.

Your Goal: To provide convincing answers to a variety of scenario-type questions.

---

[1] Competencies as listed by Michael Lombardo and Robert Eichinger, *For Your Improvement, 3rd Edition*, Minneapolis, MN: Lominger Limited, Inc., 2000.
[2] Ibid.

Your Action: Be prepared by brainstorming in advance answers to questions about competencies related to your specific area. For example, a likely question for a sales candidate would be: "Tell me about a time when you stopped trying to negotiate. What happened and what did you learn from your experience?"

Your Response: Provide a relevant example from your past to demonstrate to the interviewer your negotiating and selling skills.

Or

Suppose you have applied for a job as a senior tax accountant, and the interviewer says, "Tell me about a time when a person you supervised failed to deliver a critical work assignment. What did you do?"

Your Response might be: "As I noted on my resume, I prepare the quarterly earnings reports for my present firm. That is a very big job because, among other things, top management uses the figures to alert the board of directors about our business results before we publicly announce them. Recently, my group worked all weekend on one set of reports to finish them on time. Imagine my surprise late Sunday night when the president of the company called me at home to complain that the reports were inaccurate. He was very upset. (Go on to describe how you drove to the office, discovered your subordinate's mistake and worked all night to fix it, what you said and did about it the next day at work, what you did to make sure that mistake never happened again, and how you communicated your actions to rebuild your president's trust in your work.)

By checking out the full list of competencies and working out those most likely to apply to your next job, you can prepare yourself for questions you might be asked with regard to your workplace attitudes and behaviors.

Problem-Solving Interview

Some companies will ask you to take a test or do an exercise to see how you apply your technical skills to fix a problem. Some of these may consist of a single, short question that you answer verbally or in writing. (This is an ancient technique, so don't panic. For a hundred years, promotion from midshipman to lieutenant in the Royal Navy was based on an oral response to questions involving the handling of a sailing ship under very adverse conditions.) Some interviewers may escort you to a keyboard and ask you to compose an on-the-spot essay or to perform a take-home assignment that will require several days of research.

Your Goal: Stay calm.

Your Action: If it's a short question, do your best. If they ask for a research report and you want their job that badly, do the report.

Behavioral (Stress) Interview

There are several variations of behavioral interviews. Sometimes, an interviewer will ask you an embarrassing or an annoying question or frequently interrupt you, just to see how you react. Sometimes the interviewer will simply stop talking, to see what you will do or say to fill up the silence. These are not common interview techniques but they are very stressful. These are also unfair and, in our opinion, not very professional, even though they are not being done to make you fail. But these are techniques some interviewers use. (See "Interview No. 2: Too Much Information," Chapter 6.)

Your Goal: Stay calm.

Your Response: Smile a lot. Ask for clarification as needed. Sample: "Take off my shoes? Okay." Better response: "Sure. You can go first." If confronted with cold, stony silence, sit quietly, look pleasant, and try not to fidget. Perhaps you remember the staring game from elementary school? Whoever looked away first, lost. Exactly the same thing is going on here and in our opinion, it's an equally child-like technique. Perhaps you need to ask yourself why you want to work for an outfit that treats potential employees this way.

CHAPTER 6

LESSONS LEARNED: SOME ACTUAL INTERVIEWS

I am giving you the right answers! You are just asking the wrong questions.

—Dennis the Menace

Okay, now you're ready for a test-drive. We've collected ten sample interviews to give you a flavor of the endless possibilities you may encounter. These examples will help you avoid tripping over some of the more obvious tree roots in the career-search forest. And guess what? We didn't have to make up any of these examples. All of them happened to somebody just like you. As you will see, some of these interviews turned out just fine. Others are disasters. The world being what it is, you can count on some of each in your own personal job search. But don't sweat it. If you screw up the first time, or things don't go as smoothly as you might like, you'll have other chances to get it right. Practice will help.

Interview No. 1:
The Telephone Pre-Screen

A lot of people start their careers in sales. Selling is one of the few job positions where innate ability and a quick mind are far more important than formal education. You can't learn how to sell in a classroom. Professional selling is developed only through hands-on experience. In this example, a recruiter is screening an experienced sales person. If the candidate (we'll call him Mike) appears to meet the company's technical qualifications, and if his salary requirements fall within the range the company is prepared to pay, Mike will be asked to come in for an interview. (For more information on telephone pre-screens, see Chapters 5 and 7.)

> **RECRUITER:** You seem to have the qualifications we are looking for. Would you like to come in next week for an interview?
>
> **MIKE:** Can I ask you a few questions first to make sure the job is a good fit?
>
> **RECRUITER:** Sure.
>
> **MIKE:** What is the starting salary?
>
> **RECRUITER:** This position pays a base of $20,000 plus commission. Does that sound agreeable to you? (*Many sales jobs are straight commission. All the expenses in these jobs come out of your own pocket. It can take two or three months to fill your income pipeline while you learn the ropes, and in the meantime, you will earn nothing. A recruiter won't tell you this.*)
>
> **MIKE:** What sales quota do you expect your new people to hit in their first year?
>
> **RECRUITER:** Our more experienced sales representatives averaged $60,000 last year. That includes commission and bonus. (*He hasn't really answered the question, but for Mike's*

purposes this may be close enough for now. If Mike decides to go for an interview, he can do some more probing.)

MIKE: Does that include benefits?

RECRUITER: We offer medical and dental benefits, 401(k) with a 10 percent company match, and two weeks vacation with pay.

MIKE: Is this a full-time position?

RECRUITER: Yes. Our people work forty-hour weeks, but we do require some overtime at the end of every month. However, we allow our people to set their own hours, as long as the phones are covered.

MIKE: Does this include a company car and expense account?

RECRUITER: We don't provide a company car, but we have a car allowance. And we have an expense account for personal meals and lodging for business travel. The company will pay all your cell phone expenses, provide business cards and an office, and, on top of your base salary and commission, you can also earn a monthly bonus.

MIKE: I am very interested in coming to see you to talk more about this job.

RECRUITER: Great!

Lesson Learned: The recruiter was unusually forthcoming in this screen interview because Mike was a great candidate. Note that Mike didn't really want all the details of the job, but he did need to know if it was full- or part-time and if it was straight commission. He also needed to know how much the job paid because no candidate with experience is going to waste time going for an interview without knowing the salary range. Mike kept asking questions because it was obvious that the recruiter

(*continued on p. 36*)

(*continued from p. 35*)
was clearly interested in him, and he was willing to answer all Mike's questions. Besides, it never hurts to ask. As they say in Texas, "If you don't ask, you won't get."

Here is another screening interview, this time for a call-center sales position. The candidate has no experience.

RECRUITER: I've received your resume for the call-center representative, and we're setting up interviews for next week. (*Not a good start. This recruiter has just admitted this is a "cattle call," and you are one of many sheep to be sheared. When you show up for the interview, there could be eight other people waiting ahead of you. That is an absolute no-no from the recruiting side. A smart recruiter would have made you feel as if you were the only candidate for this job.*)

SMART RECRUITER: I've received your resume, and I'd like to set up an interview for you with the hiring manager for next week.

CANDIDATE: Oh, great! That sounds good. Uh, could you tell me a little bit more about the position? (*Perhaps you sent your resume to this company months ago, and you have no idea what job the recruiter is referring to. Many career consultants will tell you to keep a job log, but that's nonsense. When you've mass-mailed resumes, you can't keep logs. Besides, if you're like most people, you tailored your resume to fit the job you applied for. And not all positions have job descriptions.*)

RECRUITER: Sure. (*Another moron, she thinks to herself, for not reading the job description. She reads the description in a bored voice.*)

CANDIDATE: Yes, that sounds like something I would be interested in. (*Not so fast. Before you agree to go to the interview, you want to know what it pays.*)

CANDIDATE: Can you tell me what this position pays? Is it hourly or salaried?

RECRUITER: It pays between $11.50 and $13.00 an hour. (*Okay, now you know what it pays. If you can live on this wage, go for it.*)

But what if she says:

RECRUITER: I don't know what it pays. I'm just scheduling appointments for the hiring manager. (*That might be true. Her goal is to get a lot of warm bodies to this interview. But you have goals too. Let's suppose one of your goals is to avoid a commute that consumes more than two gallons of gas. Because you have researched call centers, you know that their turnover is astronomically high because these are burn-out jobs. You decide to push the recruiter for a little more data.*)

CANDIDATE: Well, I understand, but I'd really appreciate it if you could find out the salary range for me and then call me back so we can talk about scheduling an interview.

Lesson Learned: The recruiter either will agree to your deal or she won't. Life is full of surprises so you won't know until you ask. Will you operate this smoothly during your own screening interview? Probably not. You'll definitely need to practice. But it's not that hard, since you have only two possible answers to prepare for.

38

Interview No. 2: Too Much Information

Of course you want to make a good impression during your interview. Who doesn't? But giving us too much information can hurt you. Keep it strictly professional. This is a good place to mention that there is a very infamous interview technique some recruiters will use to get you to spill the beans. It's called behavioral interviewing because the recruiter is playing with your mind, trying to throw you off your game.

> In a behavioral interview, the recruiter might try to stress you out with an unusual request or an embarrassing question, to see how you handle an awkward situation.

Or the recruiter might suddenly stop talking, hoping you will find the silence unbearable and fill up the emptiness with words. Then they might let you ramble on to see if you will say something they can use to disqualify you.

As far as we're concerned, recruiters who use these tactics are worse than unprofessional—they are evil, because they are playing with you like a laboratory rat, even though what they do isn't personal.

Note that in this interview, the recruiter—a manager for a local manufacturing plant with a great reputation—doesn't intentionally use the behavioral tactic of silence, but he has a lapse of concentration that amounts to the same thing. Note also that because of desperation or desire, the applicant attempts to bargain with the recruiter. There is a proper place for negotiations, and we'll discuss that later on. But the initial interview is never that place.

MANAGER: You seem to have some inside sales experience. That's great.

CANDIDATE: What's really great is your company's reputation. I really want to work here. Tell you what. If you hire me, I'll have the company logo tattooed on my arm.

MANAGER: (*He is looking out the window at nothing in particular, thinking about how neat it would be to have a photo of the candidate with the company's logo tattooed on his arm on the front page of the plant newsletter. While he turns the thought over in his mind, he unwittingly allows the interview to lapse into a lengthy silence.*)

CANDIDATE: (*He is worried that the plant manager is looking at his expensive car in the visitors' parking area. He is afraid he won't get hired because the manager thinks he has too much money.*) That's not really my car.

MANAGER: Huh? What?

CANDIDATE: That silver Porsche isn't mine. It belongs to my girlfriend.

MANAGER: Your girl drives a Boxster? Wow! What year make is that?

CANDIDATE: I'd have to look at the owner's card in the glove box to be sure. I saw it when I was putting my brass knuckles in there.

MANAGER: You have brass knuckles in the glove box?

CANDIDATE: And some Ninja throwing stars. I figured if I left them out on the seat, somebody might get hurt.

Will Mr. Ninja Stars be hired? Would you hire him?

Lesson Learned: Get to the point as quickly as possible. Keep it business-like. Don't offer unrelated information or personal opinions. We don't care about you enough yet to want to know so much about you. After you have answered our questions, smile and shut up. Of course, if you have a skill or experience that makes you a great candidate and the interviewer fails to ask you about it, do take charge of the situation and bring up the subject yourself.

(*continued on p. 40*)

(*continued from p. 39*)

As you saw in this disaster of an interview, when the flow of conversation stopped, there was a natural tendency to want to fill up the silence with words. That is why this interviewing technique works. Giving you the silent treatment is supposed to make you feel uncomfortable so you'll spill your guts. While this is a technique that some recruiters use, it's certainly fair *and* wise to ask yourself: If treating people badly is this company's policy, why do I want to work here?

Interview No. 3: Not Ready for Prime Time

This applicant is applying for a position as a professional truck driver. He did not research the hiring company. He is overconfident, aggressive, and unprepared. And he has personal grooming issues. Fortunately in this case for our applicant, actual experience is far more important than formal education or a neat resume. And because turnover among professional drivers nationally is extremely high (100 percent at some companies), the recruiter is going to be extremely patient with this fellow, especially if he has a clean driving record.

RECRUITER: Hello, I'm Mary. Won't you sit down?

CANDIDATE: How come there's no coffee, little lady?

RECRUITER: I'm afraid that perk disappeared a long time ago. Let's get started. Your application says you were a truck driver for the federal government.

CANDIDATE: I can't talk about it much, little lady. It was top secret.

RECRUITER: Check. What sort of freight did you handle?

CANDIDATE: I mostly hauled nuclear weapons.

RECRUITER: Unfortunately, there's not much demand for that sort of cargo handling skill right now. How are your computer skills?

CANDIDATE: My what?

RECRUITER: Our drivers use on-board computers. Can you use a computer?

CANDIDATE: No, but I'm a very good driver. I had to be. Check it out.

RECRUITER: We did. We have a courier opening that might suit you. Delivering documents to banks.

CANDIDATE: That might be okay.

RECRUITER: You can keep the earrings. But you'll have to get rid of your ponytail and shave your beard. How do you feel about that?

CANDIDATE: Cut my hair? Shave my beard?

RECRUITER: You can't walk into a bank lobby looking like the captain of a pirate ship.

CANDIDATE: I look that good, huh? Will you go out with me?

Lesson Learned: Will he get the job? Probably. Will Mary go out with him? Definitely note.

Interview No. 4: Thinking Outside the Box

When confronted by overwhelmingly superior forces, clever (or desperate) generals attempt asymmetrical warfare—striking where the enemy least expects an attack. Why not try this tactic in your own interview? It won't be easy to turn the tables on us because we've seen and heard just about everything. But if you succeed, we'll certainly remember you. There's no better way to stand out from the rest of the crowd.

RECRUITER: Our clients own their own businesses, and they are very successful—and very wealthy. They also tend to be very independent thinkers. To speak plainly, our clients are used to having things their own way, and they can be very intimidating individuals. That's why we're looking for bright people with good negotiation skills. People who can think on their feet. The hardest part of this job—the most critical part—is making sure our policies are carried out without offending our clients. It's a huge challenge.

CANDIDATE: I'm sure it is. Part of my previous job involved responsibility for getting media exposure for new recording artists represented by our agency. This included country and western, hip-hop, and rap personalities. As you might imagine, the hip-hop and rap musicians were very counter-culture and extremely difficult to handle. To be utterly frank, their behavior was outrageous. In many cases, they just didn't know how to act around ordinary people. Teaching them acceptable public behavior without giving offense was part of my job. That's why I believe I'm a good candidate for this position.

RECRUITER: We've found our best field people have a great sense of humor. Tell me a story. Go ahead. Make me laugh.

CANDIDATE: Make you laugh? Sure. (*The candidate smiles, rises from her chair, walks around the recruiter's desk, steps behind him, reaches down, and tickles him lightly under both arms.*)

Lesson Learned: Yes, she got the job! Was this a dangerous thing to do? Sure it was. It was outrageous, which was why it succeeded. Yes, it could have gone horribly wrong. We're not suggesting you need to take unnecessary risks. Nobody wants to hire a potential bomb-thrower. On the other hand, some firms really do welcome candidates with initiative. One very successful sales manager for a Fortune 50 firm reported to work on the strength of a casual conversation he had with a corporate recruiter on campus. He did not have an appointment for an interview, but the day after he graduated from college, he moved his furniture and his family to his new city, put on his best business suit, and showed up in the recruiter's corporate office. The firm loved his audacity and put him to work right away. Today he handles the firm's biggest customer account, worth more than $80 million in annual revenue. So you never know. If it feels right, go with the flow.

Interview No. 5: The Trick Question

You have researched, prepared, practiced in front of a mirror (not a bad idea!), driven a hundred miles to the company of your choice, met the hiring manager, and exchanged some quick pleasantries. Now you're ready to be grilled like a cheese sandwich. How could you possibly know the interview would consist of a single trick question? Yes, we agree with you; this is outrageous behavior. And no, you didn't deserve to be ambushed. Nobody deserves that. But as we have already indicated, life is unfair and no more so than during something as subjective as the hiring process. Please note in the example that a hiring manager did this, not a corporate recruiter. We would never do that. Our job is to hire you, not trot out the firing squad.

MANAGER: What is a split infinitive?*

CANDIDATE: Huh?

MANAGER: Thanks for coming in.

Interview over.

Lesson Learned: If our hiring manager had been hiring a creative writing professor, it might be legitimate to test the applicant's knowledge of language structure. But he wasn't hiring English teachers or an editor for *Time* magazine. He was hiring an entry-level creative designer, straight out of art school. A better gauge of this applicant's quality might be to request graded samples of school projects or published work. If writing plays a prominent role in this position, it might have been a good idea to ask if the applicant had studied Latin.

(*continued on p. 46*)

---

* An infinitive consists of the word "to" and a verb, as in "to ride" or "to recycle." A split infinitive occurs when words are inserted between <u>to</u> and the verb, as in: "I want you <u>to right now recycle</u> those bottles." But you knew that, didn't you?

(continued from p. 45)

(Latin is a terrific indicator of an expanded vocabulary, since so many English words have Latin roots). Or the manager might simply have invited the candidate to audition by writing a short paragraph on the spot.

To be fair to this manager, he sought to narrow the field of candidates quickly and painlessly (for him, that is). He would probably have eventually discussed such job competencies as ethics and values, conflict management, learning on the march, handling ambiguity, comfort around senior management, etc., with anyone who managed to survive his pop quiz. But what he did in this case was to turn the formal interview process into Trivial Pursuit. This sort of thing won't happen more than once in our company, not if we get wind of it. But what goes on in academia or in a privately owned firm is another story.

> There will probably always be a few renegade hiring managers who ask applicants such thoughtful questions as who is Julio Iglesias or which of the eight Henrys led the English to victory at Agincourt.

Consider yourself fortunate for not getting this particular job. Why would you want to work for a supervisor who dispenses summary executions based on a trifle? More to the point: What other interesting, quirky short-cuts might an employee be subject to once he ships out with this New Age Captain Bligh?

Interview No. 6: We're Arrogant, and We're Ganging Up on You

There is another kind of ambush-type interview that starts by inviting the candidate into a conference room. This is sometimes referred to as a group or a "tag-team" interview. (For more information, see "Group Interview," Chapter 5.) In this particular example, there are thirteen chairs around the conference table and twelve of them are filled with people who intend to gang-tackle the candidate all at once. Quasi-governmental institutions (schools, business trade associations, and other not-for-profit bureaucracies) are especially notorious for this tactic because nobody in these organizations is really in charge. The only person actually empowered to make decisions is the chief executive. And even that person's decisions usually aren't final until the organization's board of directors gives its blessing.

> Another thing to keep in mind when interviewing with these outfits is that most of them are hostile to change and personal initiative. They are dedicated to defending the status quo.

Even the so-called activist organizations—whose chief assault weapon in formulating public policy is the lawsuit—manage to achieve the same goal of the institutions they are suing, which is to slow everything down to a standstill.

And here's a final bit of caution for you: These folks often interview candidates for *different* positions at the same sitting. They've been in this room all day talking to strangers, and they're tired and hungry. And on top of that, only some of them will actually be qualified to ask an intelligent question about your particular skills. Their titles may also not make sense to you even though the position you're interviewing for probably reports to one of them. In that case, your best bet is to make as much eye contact with everyone as possible and direct your replies to the person who just finished speaking.

FIRST SUPERVISOR: (*Addressing the others*) Mr. Schofield has applied for the position of audio-visual supervisor. Mr. Schofield currently is a producer for a TV news station in Roanoke.

SECOND SUPERVISOR: My sister lives in Roanoke.

THIRD SUPERVISOR: According to your resume, you are perfectly qualified for our position of media director. Why didn't you apply for that job?

FOURTH SUPERVISOR: That job hasn't been posted yet.

FIFTH SUPERVISOR: Really? I had better have another little chat with Mrs. Watkins over in Administration. I wonder what else they're behind on?

SIXTH SUPERVISOR: What exactly does a producer do?

CANDIDATE: I work with the assignment editor who provided the original story idea. I talk to the individuals who will be featured on camera if we decide to run with the story. Then I talk to the news editor to see how the story fits in with the other stories we might be working on. For example, our broadcast area runs more than two hundred miles, so we wouldn't want to send two crews to cover different events in the same geography, not if one crew could do both events. After the editor assigns a crew, if it's a big story, I'll go with them and direct the shoot. I edit the tape to fit the allotted time block and write the news copy for the anchor. If it's our lead story, I'll prepare a five-second tape teaser for the lead-in to the news.

SEVENTH SUPERVISOR: A teaser?

CANDIDATE: To tease your interest. To keep you from changing channels. (*Imitates announcer's voice*) 'Tornado strikes elementary school! Film at eleven.'

EIGHTH SUPERVISOR: I never watch TV.

NINTH SUPERVISOR: So the anchor reads your copy? That's all they do?

CANDIDATE: Sometimes they write some of their own material. But they can't write the entire newscast themselves. On a big story, they might accompany the crew to the scene and do a live stand-up.

TENTH SUPERVISOR: (*Impressed*) Sounds like you're a one-man band.

CANDIDATE: Actually, I have a lot of help. There are three other producers, three assistant producers, six editors, four assistant editors, a dozen technicians, and the helicopter pilot. But we're all behind the scenes. Everybody's news is about the same, just like the weather is the same for everybody. It's the on-air personality that viewers tune in to see.

ELEVENTH SUPERVISOR: That weather girl on Channel 4 is a riot with that big plastic finger she uses. She was at the mall yesterday, giving fingers to everyone.

TWELFTH SUPERVISOR: Why are you interested in this position?

CANDIDATE: Several reasons. I'm at the top of my profession in Roanoke. I'd like to be news editor, but there's no sign of anyone retiring soon so there's nowhere else for me to go unless I move to a bigger market. But even if I move, I'll probably still be a producer until I prove myself all over again. Since I've learned all I can, it's time to think about something different. This job sounds challenging and since it's a new job, in many ways I'd be setting my own standards. I like that. As you know, I majored in education, so I'm sure you'd be satisfied with any training materials I might be asked to create. And if I may speak frankly, producers aren't very well compensated, considering we routinely work ten hours a day. This job pays a lot better. And finally, this is my hometown. My parents and my wife's parents are here.

SECOND SUPERVISOR: We never pay moving expenses.

THIRD SUPERVISOR: (*Stubbornly*) I still think you ought to apply for the media director's job.

NINTH SUPERVISOR: A consultant suggested we purchase a new camera since we've just moved to digital editing. What do you think about that?

CANDIDATE: Well, you know what a consultant is. Somebody who borrows your watch to tell you what time it is.

ALL SUPERVISORS EXCEPT NUMBER NINE: (*Laughing*)

NINTH SUPERVISOR: But seriously. His advice on other important matters was spot on.

CANDIDATE: But that's exactly why you lent him your watch in the first place. Because you needed to know what time it was.

ALL SUPERVISORS, INCLUDING NUMBER NINE: (*Laughing*)

FIRST SUPERVISOR: (*Still laughing*) Thank you very much, Mr. Schofield, for coming in. We'll be in touch.

Lesson Learned: Schofield successfully paddled his canoe through some very dangerous waters. He ignored the irrelevant crosstalk and answered perfectly the few questions that were raised about his qualifications. He deflected one supervisor's praise by giving much of the credit to others—thus signaling that his primary loyalty is to his organization—an enormously important personal trait in any bureaucracy. Likewise, he refused to endorse the implied criticism of his news anchor—

(*continued on p. 51*)

(*continued from p. 50*)

even though agreeing might have gained him an ally. This way he demonstrated an inclusive leadership style as opposed to a dividing-and-conquering style. And by emphasizing the anchor's important contributions, he further demonstrated his loyalty. He artfully used humor to avoid taking a position on the consultant's recommendation, which means nobody here is mad at him. And he made everybody laugh—twice. Schofield's performance was world-class. He will almost certainly be offered the position.

A much more sophisticated version of this type of interview is the panel interview. The candidate sits down in front of a three-person panel. The first person asks all the questions. The second person acts as scribe and takes notes. The third person's job is to read the candidate's body language.

The important question for you is: How comfortable would you be with these people? Do you like this environment? Is it professional? Is extra money a major consideration for you? It shouldn't be. All you will do is hurt yourself—and hurt the firm, if your primary motivator is money. Always listen to your gut. If you're uneasy, don't take the job. There's always another job.

Interview No. 7: Dress for Success

There are interviews, and there are interviews. This hiring manager is an art director for a large advertising agency. The agency has run an ad for "young suburban women in business casual clothing" to participate as extras in a TV commercial. The compensation is minimal, but some of the candidates are hoping this might be their stepping stone into a motion picture career. (See Chapter 8 for more information on how to dress for an interview.)

> **DIRECTOR:** (*Frazzled*) Next! Your name?
>
> **CANDIDATE:** Marcia.
>
> **DIRECTOR:** (*Impatient*) Pick up the bag, Marcia, and walk from the X on the floor over to the desk. Stay in the light. Now put the bag on the desk and turn around. Good. Walk over to me. Slowly. Smile. Hands at your sides. Good Lord, girl! That mini-skirt is way too short. And those net stockings! We're selling a food product here, not memberships in a strip club.
>
> **CANDIDATE:** But your ad said 'business casual' clothes.
>
> **DIRECTOR:** Yes, it did. What business are you in? Next!

> **Lesson Learned:** In this case, the candidate literally failed to dress for the part she wanted. Check out Chapter 7 for hints about dressing for the position. Remember, dress for the job you want, not the job you have.

Interview No. 8: What's Legal and What's Not

Nobody is allowed to ask you a personal question during your interview unless it relates to the job. For instance, if the position calls for extensive travel, or if there are certain physical requirements, it's perfectly acceptable to ask a candidate how either of those things might affect them. If the position calls for a lot of walking around dangerous moving machinery, that will be the candidate's cue to mention his wooden leg, or the fact that she is legally blind in one eye. But no fishing expeditions are allowed. We can't ask you if you're pregnant, or if you've ever had a serious illness, for example. Gratuitous comments about your physical appearance are also off limits. However, some managers play by their own rules:

HIRING MANAGER: Well, young lady. I can see by your ring that you're married. Do you plan to start a family soon?

Or

HIRING MANAGER: We work hard but we also play hard. And when we play we like to have fun. Are you fun?

Or

HIRING MANAGER: The last person to hold this job went through a terrible divorce. It took three years. And during that time he wasn't worth powder enough to blow himself up. You're not planning to get a divorce, are you?

Or

HIRING MANAGER: A big part of this job involves traveling to our West Coast branches every five or six weeks. If you have children, what provisions do you or your spouse make for childcare when you will be out of town for three or four days? (Note: It's okay to ask about travel; not okay to ask about children.)

Or

HIRING MANAGER: I had to fire the person you will be replacing because he handed out religious tracts on the sidewalk during his breaks, and he annoyed our customers with his preaching. What is your religion?

Know your rights. Know what's legal, and what's not. Ask yourself: How badly do I want this job?

Legal questions include: Your qualifications, job skills, education, career goals, your address and telephone number, your ability to travel, your strengths and weaknesses.

You may refuse to answer questions about: Your marriage, your children, your parents, your spouse, your age and weight, your finances, religion, and health, whether you own or rent your home, and who you live with.

If someone stares at you or makes you uncomfortable, that's a clue. This manager knows he's breaking the law—either he doesn't care or he thinks he can bluff his way out of trouble.

Unless you plan to walk out of the interview, you'll have to answer his question. Do you like this person enough to work for him even if he's an ass?

Another question: Is this your first job or your seventh? If you're coming straight out of school into a tough job market, you might want to take the job, after you assess your ability to roll with the punches. An experienced candidate who knows she's a valuable asset will know better than that. To further complicate your decision, managerial asses are often very complex people. Many are world-class jerks that enjoy pushing subordinates around. Others, beneath a grumpy exterior, may be caring and compassionate people who will treat you like the son or daughter they never had. Like so many of the other choices we make in our lives, this one is a judgment call.

Interview No. 9: Curveball

This interview has progressed very nicely. The candidate has applied for a marketing position with a great local company and after only ten minutes, she and the hiring manager are chatting away like long-lost friends. But then the manager delivers this bolt from the blue:

> **MANAGER:** I should probably mention that one of the responsibilities of this position—and I know it's a little unusual—is that the marketing manager oversees all our financial publications. That includes producing the 10K, 10Q, and quarterly statements to shareholders and, of course, the annual report.
>
> **CANDIDATE:** Oh, dear. I'm a marketing major, not a finance major. I'd really like to work for you in marketing, but to be perfectly honest, I just don't want to do financial communications.
>
> **MANAGER:** Well. Thanks for being honest with me.

Lesson Learned: This was a heartbreaker for both parties, but honesty in this case was definitely the right policy. Why would you take a job you know you're going to hate, or a job for which you lack a critical skill?

Interview No. 10: There's Never a Lawyer around When You Need One

Private companies often have several owners—some of whom may be silent partners while others handle day-to-day operations. This hiring manager, who is also part-owner in the firm, obviously thinks he is either General George Patton or super-spy James Bond. He also appears to be ethically challenged. But that isn't the only thing that's going on here. Keep in mind that anything can happen when two individuals—in this case, you and the hiring manager—maneuver freely to learn more about each other. Note how the applicant handles each of the bombastic manager's outrageous statements with a very professional attempt to redirect the interview back to her job search—a task that is really the manager's responsibility.

MANAGER: We've grown about 25 percent each year for the past five years. But we could do a lot better if our promotions, catalog, and advertising groups were on the same page. That's why we're looking for a marketing director. Someone who can bring focus to our whole operation. You know, tie everything together. We think we should be growing at a 40 percent rate. Maybe higher.

CANDIDATE: I'd like to be part of a program that ambitious.

MANAGER: Ambitious? Ha! We're already the biggest player in our market. One day we'll be the only player. We still have three large competitors, but not for long.

CANDIDATE: I saw a hospital study that rated your product very highly. What is the greatest single factor behind your remarkable growth?

MANAGER: You read that Florida study? Good girl! Then you know we've got the best product. Everybody says so. And we pay our people very well, so they're loyal as hell. They're the best. Nobody ever quits on us. But it's our ads that keep us out in front of the pack. We advertise directly to the clinical specialists who prescribe our product. Testimonials from satisfied patients. Great stuff. Works every time. And if they don't say exactly what we want them to, we do a little doctoring of our own.

CANDIDATE: Excuse me?

MANAGER: We put words in their mouth. We make it up. Besides, it's probably what they would say if they really thought about it. It's all perfectly legal. We get them to approve the ads. Most of our users are low income or retired blue collar. Nobody ever paid any attention to them before. They're happy to do it. We don't even have to pay them.

CANDIDATE: I read some of your ads. They're like little biographies. Quite wonderful stories, really. Wherever do you find such great examples of case studies?

MANAGER: We have a little arrangement with some of the clinics.

CANDIDATE: (*Shocked*) The specialists?

MANAGER: (*Laughing*) We'd never ask medical professionals to compromise themselves. Our agreement is with the clerical people. Don't worry. It's all up and up.

CANDIDATE: I researched two of your competitors. They hardly advertise at all.

MANAGER: Did you, now? That's exactly the sort of initiative we're looking for. Can you keep a secret?

CANDIDATE: Me? Sure.

MANAGER: We maintain complete surveillance on all our major competitors. They don't do anything without our knowing about it—in fact, sometimes we know what they'll do *before* they do it.

CANDIDATE: Really.

MANAGER: Let's just say we hear things. Take it from me. They're history.

Lesson Learned: Sounds like this applicant could be on the inside track, if she wants to work for Mr. Covert Operations. Would you want to work for him? Why or why not?

As we said earlier, we didn't have to make up interviews like these. There are plenty more where these came from. Your interview won't go as badly as some of these, or so we hope. And it probably won't be nearly as interesting as this last one. But the point is—anything can happen and it probably will, sooner or later. Be prepared to roll with the punches. If you suddenly find yourself up to your sprockets in lemons during an interview, don't panic. Make lemonade. By the bushel if necessary. Remember, if you're skilled and experienced in your field, our questions probably won't eliminate you. But everything else might.

CHAPTER 7

THE PRE-SCREEN AND PHONE INTERVIEW

Put your faith in the Lord, but keep your powder dry.
—Oliver Cromwell

If we like your resume, we'll call and we'll probably also e-mail you. We'll want to pre-screen you first to determine if we want to talk to you again. We won't ask you a lot of questions during a pre-screen. It's mostly to tell you that we're interested in you. We want to know if you're still available. If you live outside normal commuting range, we want to know if you would consider moving to our town.

We also want to know your salary expectations.

Please don't tell us salary is negotiable. That's true, to a point, but most jobs have a salary range and the range itself is never negotiable.

Be prepared to give us your salary requirement. We can't bring you in for an interview without it.

If you seem to be a good fit, then we will set up a time to talk. If you aren't at home, we'll leave a message. Don't call us back a dozen times. Leave one voicemail. If you don't hear from us by the end of the next day, it's okay to call us again one more time. But don't wait a week to get back to us, either.

When we telephone for an interview at the time you select, try to be prepared. Don't excuse yourself to run somewhere else in your house or out to your car to collect your resume or other materials. Have whatever documents you need next to the phone. If we hear the TV or radio or power equipment blasting away in the background while we talk, guess what? You won't be coming to see us.

Barking dogs or screaming children in the background are probably additional indications that your life is out of control.

Of course we're mothers and dads, too. We know there are family emergencies that cannot be prevented. If we called you at a really bad time, don't give us the gory details about how your toilet is overflowing into your downstairs neighbor's apartment or how your dog just died. Just apologize immediately and ask: "Can we set up another time to talk?"

(See Chapter 6 for an example of a telephone pre-screen interview.)

CHAPTER 8

CLOTHES STILL MAKE THE MAN (OR WOMAN)

You can observe a lot just by watching.

—Yogi Berra

It's a sad fact, but some of today's job applicants are social barbarians. Some don't know how to dress properly for an interview, and some don't even know which fork to use at supper. We'll get to dining habits later, but first we have three words about clothing. And those three words are: Dress your best.

Dress your best because we want to see what you look like at your best. Whatever we actually want you to wear when you come to work for us is a totally different story.

Men

Dress for the position you want, not the job you already have. If you interview for the post of auto mechanic, you wouldn't arrive at the body shop in a three-piece suit; you would probably wear khakis and a shirt with a collar. If you are being interviewed by a bank or a retail store, dress like a banker or a salesclerk. When in doubt, it's always better to be overdressed. But whatever you wear, it had better be pressed and clean.

Even if you are being interviewed by a laid-back dot.com type (if you can find one that is still hiring), dress up. The fat guy with a beard, ragged shorts, and ratty old sneakers behind the big desk may be the owner of the company, but he will appreciate style, whether he has any of his own or not.

For men, no jewelry, except for a watch and your wedding ring. That also means no earrings. The assembly line and the construction industry won't care, but for the business work-place, nose rings and tattoos are unacceptable and distracting.

A clean shave is mandatory.

Beards are out (unless you're applying for a college professorship—and then all your dean will want to see is your PhD and published works).

Your hair should be clean and groomed. Long hair is out—for men and women.

Many large corporations, banks, and small professional firms like law offices and accounting firms are still very conservative about clothing and personal grooming. In fact, many formerly freewheeling businesses are becoming steadily more conservative in dress because employees are embarrassing management by abusing their business-casual dress privileges. In many firms, even neatly groomed shoulder-length hair is no longer considered suitable for a professional woman. If that sounds too old-fashioned for you, try to remember that the public wants its attorneys and bankers to look like responsible adults, not schoolgirls or carnival-ride operators.

We're not asking you to cut your hair for us, but it had better be tied back. Dandruff is a gross-out. And speaking of hair, if you have a cat, don't bring us samples.

We expect to see a clean suit jacket with matching trousers. Your suit should not smell of mothballs. Corporations and small professional offices (lawyers, architects, doctors) will also want to see a tie. If you elect to go tie-less, wear a dress shirt and jacket. If you're wearing a tie and everybody else is in shorts or overalls, ask what their dress code is. That way, if you survive the initial interview and get invited back for a serious talk with the hiring manager, you'll be able to blend in better.

We will never judge you on the style or brand of your shoes because you may be wearing only what you can afford. But we deduct major points for mud, dirt, and dust because everybody can afford shoe polish.

Women

Dress your best. Wear a skirt that falls below the knee or dress pants that match your suit. No dresses, sundresses, Capris, culottes, tank tops, or anything that reveals your shoulders. Tone down the colors. Black is best; gray and brown are fine. Never wear shorts or a mini-skirt.

Don't use perfume. Many people are allergic to it. Besides, long after you leave our office, it will linger, making it impossible for us to ever forget you, like the smell of steamed cabbage. Makeup? Of course! But use it sparingly. Light colored lipstick or lip gloss is fine.

Large, dangling, or flashy jewelry is out of place in the workplace. Small earrings are fine. Noisy bracelets and brooches the size of hood ornaments are out; they are distracting. (If you don't believe us, look at the jewelry your favorite TV anchorwoman wears.)

We don't want to see extremely long nails and rings on every finger. How will you manage to type on your computer? (And everybody types nowadays, even the chief executive.) Leave your $25,000 solitaire ring at home. If you show up loaded down with diamonds or pearls, we're going to wonder why you need to work.

Shoes with small heels are okay but flats are better. If you're tall, you don't want to add more height; some insecure people find it intimidating to have candidates towering over them. Avoid stiletto heels, flip-flops, and sandals. Open toes are out, even with nylons. And you are wearing nylons, right? Save your net stockings for Saturday night.

If we invite you back for a second interview, congratulations! Dress just as nicely as you did for us the first time. Because the second time around, you'll be meeting different people, including some of our top managers.

One more little thing: If you enjoy dressing up and you have a stylish, expensive wardrobe, and you happen to notice everyone in our building wears a company uniform, you might not like working here.

CHAPTER 9

THE INITIAL INTERVIEW

The race is not to the swift, nor the battle to the strong, nor bread to the wise, nor riches to the intelligent, nor favor to the skillful; but time and chance happen to them all.

—Ecclesiastes 9:11

Here is some advice for you. Never be late for an interview. Internet mapping tools are great, but don't you dare depend on them alone. Your interview is far too important to be trusted to some satellite that translated a shadow cast by the late afternoon sun as an access road that exists only in virtual space. Always drive by our building in advance, preferably the day before your appointment. (Internet maps won't warn you about that torn-up street and a mile-long detour in front of our office, either.)

In a large city like Washington, D.C., or Atlanta, Georgia, there could be as many as thirty companies in one high-rise building. If you don't know which building we're in, it could be a really bad idea to stop in the middle of six lanes of Atlanta high-speed traffic to ask directions. And unless we have our own parking lot (you did ask us about parking during the screen interview, didn't you?), the maps can't tell you where to park.

Plan in advance where you are going to leave your car. If the only garage you can find is some distance from our building, you don't want to show up at our door soaking wet from the rain or sweating if you ran eight blocks in the hot sun. We notice those things. Find out in advance what floor we are on. What will you do if there's nobody in our lobby you can ask for directions? Some office lobbies have more uniformed guards than Fort Knox. Others have no human attendants and are accessed only by personal key cards. Guess which kind of lobby you'll be in if you're lost?

Here are some things we don't ever want to hear you say: "I'm running late. Traffic is terrible." Or: "I'm lost. Where are you guys located?"

If you can't even arrive on time for your first interview, what does that tell us about you? If you must be late, don't expect a happy face when you finally show up. High-level recruiters may deal with eight or ten applicants a day, and if you ruin our schedules, you're only hurting your own chances because we won't be able to give you the full time you deserve. And if we have set up sequential interviews for you, all the folks who made time available for you will be upset with us and with you for wasting their time. Be early.

A word to the wise: Don't have issues the day of your interview. Yes, we know children get sick. Pets run away. Emergencies arise. Things happen. But they better not happen the day of your interview. When you have landed that first interview with a company you are interested in, nothing is more important than keeping your appointment. Make that your mantra.

Okay, you made it to our reception area. We know you're nervous. But remember, we're not here to intimidate you—we're here to hire you. So do everyone a favor and make it easy for us to like you. Focus on the positive aspects of the situation. We believe that you're a qualified candidate—unless you lied on your resume (and we'll get to that topic later), which is why we invited you in for an interview. We've also spent a fair amount of time and money arranging to meet you, so if for no other reason than that, we plan on being very nice to you.

In the Reception Area

We'll do our best not to waste your time, so don't waste ours. Be here at the appointed time. And don't wander around our building, poking into things. Don't make us send out patrols to track you down. Stay in the reception area. And if you have to use the washroom, do it before we get started.

Don't clutter up our lobby with your baggage. You won't need your briefcase or your umbrella or a laptop or a large purse while you are visiting us. Don't bring a bag lunch. Don't make cell phone calls while you wait. What did you do before cell phones were invented?

Leave your phone in your car, because if it rings during your interview, we're going to hang up on you.

It's okay to look at the plaques and trophies in our reception area if you're bored. But don't start conversations with people walking by unless they talk to you first. You are here for one purpose—stay focused on that.

You may find yourself waiting alongside another candidate. We won't schedule both of you at the same time on purpose, but even professionals screw up once in a while. And maybe it wasn't our fault. Maybe she had to drive two hundred miles and got here early. Stuff happens. Be professional. Don't feel threatened. If it's a good job obviously other people will have applied for it.

Be nice to our receptionist. Do whatever she tells you. Be warned: We're going to ask for her impression of you when you leave.

It's easy for her to be totally honest about you, since, unlike us, she has nothing invested in the outcome.

First Impressions

Always stand up when we come out to meet you.

Make eye contact. Give us a smile. Be pleasant. First impressions, remember?

Let us decide when to shake your hand. If you initiate a handshake, it might look aggressive or even desperate.

Assertiveness is okay for a sales position; it's bad for almost everything else. And don't crush our hand or give us a sweaty palm. (Wipe your sweaty hand casually on your clothes as you stand up.)

Don't speak until spoken to. Don't make small talk about the weather. If you are soaking wet from your dash out of our parking lot, or if you're covered with ice and snow, we'll notice, and we'll apologize for the elements.

Don't ask us for directions to the restroom. (You should have asked the receptionist when you had the chance.) Don't ask us for water or coffee or an aspirin. If we offer you a drink, it's probably a good idea to accept, even if you aren't thirsty. Holding a mug will give your nervous hands something to do while we chat.

Don't chew gum.

Don't smell like cigarette smoke. And we don't want to smell your body odor, your perfume, or your aftershave, either.

CHAPTER 10

AT LAST! THE INTERVIEW AND SALARY DANCE

The day will come when even this ordeal will be sweet to remember.

—Virgil

It's okay to bring a notepad to the interview as long as you don't write down everything we say. Remember to bring enough copies of your resume to hand to everyone who interviews you. Do this *before* the interview starts. HR people will usually have your resume handy. But a manager won't have time to prepare for you; she will almost certainly have misplaced the copy we sent her last week. Don't ask us to make copies for you.

We don't expect you to know much about us. That's because we are looking at you as a whole person and not just how good you are at research (unless you applied for one of our laboratory jobs). But when we ask if you know what we do, don't tell us you didn't have time to check us out. We expect that you will have looked at our website. We expect that you did enough research to know what we do and who our major customers are and what markets we serve.

Don't waste our time by asking for a job description. Didn't you read it when you applied with us? Sad fact. Not every job comes with a written job description. All medium-sized and large companies and all government jobs will have a job description outlining the task metrics and the company's expectations for the position. As a candidate, it's critically important that you know that your new firm understands the responsibilities and account-abilities of the job you applied for. A written job description helps you to focus on what's important. Otherwise, you could spend most of your time on a new job pushing water uphill; that's to say, you could be performing tasks nobody wants done. You really don't want to take a job and then have a hiring manager tell you: "There's no job description but Suzie's been doing that job for twenty years. Suzie knows the job backwards and forwards. She can teach you what you need to know."

Yes, we know that happens a lot. But try not to let it happen to you. If there's no job description in place, it could be a lot harder for you to be successful if nobody except Suzie knows what the company expects you to do. If you are fortunate enough to be looking at two jobs, one with a job description and one where your hiring manager doesn't really know what the job is, or if she can't tell you on what basis your performance will be evaluated, maybe you should think really hard about taking the position that *has* a written job description, even if the salary is a bit less.

A lot of perfectly good entry-level jobs have no job descrip-tion, and that should not cause you undue alarm. If it's a great job, go for it. But do understand it's a potential speed bump.

Body Language

Earlier, we mentioned that it's not so much what you say that can hurt you; it's everything else about you. That includes your body language. We can tell a great deal about you even before you open your mouth.

> Reading body language is not difficult. If *you* can tell when your friends are bored, nervous, or unhappy, what kind of information do you think a really skilled interviewer will discover by looking you over?

That's why it's really important to sit up straight, smile, and look us in the eye. Don't fidget. Don't wave your hands at us when it's your turn to talk. Business people use hand gestures to emphasize key points, not to punctuate each word. Keep your hands in your lap—or wrap them around that mug of coffee we offered you before we started.

What about Tests?

If we ask you to take a test, take it. A test can be as simple as writing a short news item if you're applying for a job at a radio station. Or you may be asked to fill out some type of personality exam or IQ test. A retail store, for example, may test to see if you are basically honest or how good you will be at calming down angry customers. Some small firms, on the other hand, may ask you to do complex research requiring several days of very hard work. If you want their job that badly, do the report. Otherwise, tell them to take a hike.

Mostly, it's small, privately-owned companies who will test you, although a publicly-traded company may ask you to take a personality test after you come on board. These tests may include Myers-Briggs, Caliper, I-OPT, or Keirsey Temperament Sorter. They are intended to help you succeed and grow with us and not to disqualify you from your new job. Such tests are copyrighted and often cost hundreds of dollars apiece because they must be administered or "graded" by certified professionals. Usually we can only afford to give them to new hires, although sometimes we will administer a test to the final few candidates being considered for a position.

Some firms give pre-employment tests only to people they are really interested in. Legally speaking, we can't test for one position unless we test everybody who applies for it. Publicly-traded companies don't generally do tests. Partly, we're afraid one of you will screw up the test and decide to sue us. But mostly, we have enough other resources to check you out. Besides, we're pretty good at spotting phonies.

If you are taking a pre-employment test, you will notice that some questions have no apparent right or wrong answer. Answer these questions the way you believe the company wants you to answer. It's another mind game, so smile and play along.

Here's a clue. If you are taking a test, you'll probably be asked the same question in many different ways. In this first example, it's pretty obvious the company wants to know if you are a team player. You might be asked:

- Are you a team player?
- Do you prefer to work on a project with a group?
- Do you prefer to work on assignments by yourself?
- Do you enjoy a team environment?
- Would you rather work alone?
- When you need to get the job done quickly, would you rather do the work yourself?
- When you are working under a tight deadline, are you comfortable delegating some of the responsibilities to others?

But suppose the company wants to know if you are comfortable with ambiguity (one indication that you might be management material), or whether you prefer working within existing guidelines (one hallmark of an individual contributor). The only right answer to these questions is the answer that is right for you:

- Do you prefer to set your own goals?
- Do you prefer to work within a framework of guidelines established by others?
- Do you prefer clear direction?
- Are you comfortable establishing your own priorities?
- Do you prefer an environment where you are free to try new ideas?
- Do you prefer to work on tasks in which the limits are clearly defined?
- Are you comfortable working on projects with a high probability of failure?

Obviously the company won't make it easy for you to figure out what it is trying to do, because that would defeat the test. These look-alike questions will be sprinkled throughout your test, along with many others, and there may be still other questions that make no sense at all to you. Sample:

• Still waters run deep. True or false?

Sorry. We never did figure this one out. But it's a question from an actual test. (Hey, we never said we had ALL the answers for you.)

The Salary Dance

Here's what it's all about: Your salary. Compensation is important because although work satisfies many human needs, all of us work to live (and a very few of us actually live to work, poor souls!). But although you can't wait to tear into this section, we're going to ask you to back up and take a deep breath, especially if you turned to this part first before you read the rest of our book.

For those of you first-time job seekers who may have just entered the job market and are reading this chapter in a bookstore, we're going to ask you to sit down and have a coffee and a muffin before you read one more word. You're going to need some comfort food because you're probably going to be very unhappy with what we're going to say to you on the next couple of pages. On the other hand, if you already have a job but you're in the market for a better position, that's cool. You can keep reading. But coffee and a muffin sound pretty good to us anyhow.

Got your coffee? Good. We're going to lay a lot of hard truths on you in this chapter. We'll start with this news flash: **There's more to a job than money**. Forget about salary, especially if you are new to the job market. Your job search is not about salary or benefits. It's about getting your foot in the door. Because what you are looking for is **opportunity**.

For example, suppose your goal is to land a job with General Motors or Ford because they offer very good salaries and benefits. Nice, but in our opinion, wrong. If you have researched those companies, you know they are both losing market position. Will GM and Ford be around in ten years? Sure. But they will probably be a lot smaller, with correspondingly less career opportunities for new employees. Shrinking companies tend to have different managerial mindsets and corporate cultures (and smaller departmental budgets) than growing companies that are winning in the marketplace and gaining market share. The authors have worked for winners and losers and believe us when we say it's a lot easier to get out of bed in the morning when you work for a company that's hitting the ball out of the park every day.

Since you're probably going to be working for at least thirty years, it would be much smarter of you to look for opportunity in a growing industry that's going to be around for as long as you have to work.

For example, if you happen to like cold weather, the Canadian province of Alberta is booming with brand-new companies making petroleum from oil shale. And all those companies are hiring like crazy—engineers and heavy equipment operators, of course, but they also need sales people, training and payroll specialists, lawyers, accountants, computer programmers, secretaries, electricians, doctors, nurses, security, pilots, truckers, cooks and bakers, you name it. And guess what? We've got plenty of oil shale here in the U.S., too. Even if hydrogen fuel cells replace gasoline in twenty years, where do you think plastic comes from? And unlike gasoline, there are no alternatives in sight for plastic. Looking ahead thirty years, do you think there might be more opportunity for you in Detroit, Michigan, or Calgary, Alberta?

So here's the first hard truth: **Take whatever job you can get and work your way up**. We know that's not what you wanted to hear, because if you're a first-time job hunter, you probably have your heart set on a certain field. But what you should know is that although the job you are offered may not be your dream job, people change careers all the time. True, some people study to be teachers or finance specialists, and they work in the same school or bank all their lives. But that is uncommon behavior. People change careers because economic forces have wiped out their company, or because they have learned everything they can, or because they are bored, or because they hate their boss, or because they think the grass is greener somewhere else, or for many other reasons. We are a mobile society. Three out of every four of the people in your college class will end up in a different field than the one they prepared for in school. Want proof? A colleague of one of the authors who majored in maritime propulsion systems became a very successful advertising manager in a Fortune 50 firm. Another colleague who majored in economics is director of human resources for a manufacturing company. Still another who graduated from an agricultural college directs the mergers and acquisitions activity for a one-billion-dollar business. And a divinity school graduate creates high-tech educational exhibits. The authors of this book have degrees in retail marketing and journalism and both are now in Human Resources. Go figure.

More bad news: **You might never land a good job in your field**. It happens. Suppose we offer to pay you $22,000. Now you have a choice. Will you stay in a field you trained for, or move on? A lot of graduates are so heavily in debt that they are afraid to move outside of their specialty. Sometimes they turn down offers that might turn into something wonderful because they feel those jobs are beneath them. Suppose we offer you $12 an hour to do something boring. Maybe ours is a huge company with great potential, and you should take the job to see what happens. Maybe ours is a no-name company in a declining market, but it's your dream job. Maybe we just offered you the best job in the world, but we're going to pay you $15,000 less than you need. The only right answer is the answer that works for you.

Here's another truism for you: **Your college degree does not make you an expert**. There are only a very few career fields where you can learn everything you need to know in a classroom. You can't walk into a high-rise building right out of school and be head of security. You can't step from the classroom into a manufacturing plant and be a health and safety manager. Even if you have a working knowledge of OSHA regulations and environmental law, you don't have any experience in applying them to everyday life. Trial lawyers, purchasing managers, Human Resources and sales professionals, just to cite four career areas, learn their stuff the hard way, out in the workplace, just like ironworkers, surgeons, and coal miners. That is why most employers want to see certifications, internships, or actual work experience, especially if you are applying for an entry-level management position.

Another tough truth: Got an advanced degree? Wonderful! **But that doesn't mean we are going to offer you a great job at a great salary.** Of course, if you are a Yale or Princeton graduate, you are worth more to us than if you are coming out of a really good state university. That may not be fair, but that's the way it is. But most people don't attend Ivy League schools. So here's another truth for you: **It's not important where you went to school or whom you know. It's what is on your resume.** And that means experience.

And now for some really, really bad news. **If you are new to the job market, you probably aren't worth what you think you're worth, salary-wise.** Sorry, but that's as real and as tough as a green apple.

Most of the time, the people who don't know their real worth haven't done their homework. A lot of college graduates are totally clueless about what they are worth, and if this describes you, your first job-hunt will be an especially disappointing time, at least at first. That said, it's normal and perhaps even healthy to have certain high expectations about your self-worth. We've all read those great magazine articles about the liberal arts major with a four-year degree from some little no-name school that landed a $140,000 job with a New York City consulting firm right after graduation. But how often do you think that happens?

So here's another tough truth: **If you are a first-time job seeker, or if you have been out of the job market for a while (perhaps to raise a family), we're going to pay you as little as possible.**

Ready for more? **If you happen to be female, some companies are going to offer you less money than they would a man.** Starting salaries for women may be 10 percent to 20 percent less than starting salaries for males in a comparable job, even in this day and age. Yes, there are a few glass ceilings.

Chow down on that muffin while we explain some tough facts of life to you. Stay with us, and then we'll explain what you can do to level the playing field, a little.

If you are re-entering the job market after ten years of raising children, unless you live in a cave, you know that there have been a lot of changes in your field, whatever it was. Even if you never left the job market, if you worked in the same niche with the same firm, it's possible that your own company may not have kept pace with the best practices, the newest ideas and operating methods, and the latest technologies. If you got laid off or surplused or outsourced or right-sized or some other corporate euphemism for a mass firing, this may be why you're walking the pavement and waiting for us to call you in for an interview. While you or your company stayed in a comfortable rut, the world moved on, and suddenly you and your firm were obsolete.

If this has happened to you, you are almost in the same position as a candidate who just graduated from college and is in the job market for the first time. That's to say, your work experience may no longer be relevant.

What are we saying? We're saying experience counts a lot, *but only if it's up-to-date.* A word to the wise and to the currently employed: Invest in yourself. Didn't we warn you on the very first page that the good old days when a paternalistic company would look after you forever are history?

So what are you worth to the company of your choice, really? It's not that hard to find out. Think about what happens when you go shopping for a new car. Smart car buyers know what the dealer paid for a car before they go in to the showroom. A smart shopper hands the invoice she printed from the Internet to the first sales person she sees. Car salespeople may hate it when you do that, but if they want your business, they have to deal with you, and they have to give you their best deal or you're going to go to a competitor.

What you have to remember is that looking for a job *is* a job. It's hard work. We have already mentioned the "salary finder" web sites. (See "Some Advice on Internet Job Sites," Chapter 2.) These are tools, but we don't have a lot of confidence in them. Some websites may tell you that you are worth a great deal of money, but just remember that those websites are not going to pay you a salary. You have to be realistic. Especially when you're just starting out, you're always going to get the low end of the range, especially if you aren't in a major market.

Suppose you are a computer programmer in Des Moines, Iowa, where the cost of living and housing is considered relatively low. Different regions tend to use different combinations of computer programs, but let's suppose the exact same job is available in New York City. Your Des Moines position might pay $40,000. The comparable New York job might pay $60,000. But before you pack your bags and head for the Big Apple, remember that New York is a high-cost, high-tax town. Sad to say, $100,000 is considered to be barely a middle-class income in New York City these days.

If you want to know about salaries, do your homework just as you would for that new car you're going to buy! Go to the library. Surf the Internet. Read business publications like *Fortune* and *Business Week* and the *Wall Street Journal* and newspaper articles about your field. Talk to your college career advisors. They can tell you what the average starting offer is for graduates in an entry-level job, and what you can expect to earn in ten years. Talk with professors who have actually worked in your field. Attend college job fairs. Most medium-size and all large companies offer paid or unpaid student internships. Shame on you if you failed to take advantage of a learning opportunity to get some real-world experience—and to get noticed by that company. (A lot of internships generate job offers because companies like to try before they buy.) Ask questions of your friends and peers who are already employed. Ask your family to refer you to people you can talk to. Do you know anybody in Human Resources? Did you check out the trade association website for your field? If you know you will be in Washington, D.C., where most trade groups are located, pick up the phone and make an appointment. In many cases, somebody will be delighted to meet with you. Bottom line: Interview us, before we interview you.

Okay, let's get back to your telephone screening interview. At some firms and in all government jobs, the salary range[1] is posted, along with a brief job description. If the salary is posted, we're not going to bring that up during your interview, since you already know what it is.

If the salary is not posted, at some point during your interview we're going to ask you about your salary requirements. If you're straight out of school, that can be a very intimidating question. But the salary question doesn't have to be an awkward dance,

---

[1]Depending on the salary band a position falls into, an average range might be from $7,000 to $10,000. Jobs in the highest salary bands will have a much wider range, and these jobs usually come with extra goodies: performance bonuses, stock options, and profit-sharing.

although it often starts out that way.

Don't tell us to leave that topic in the parking lot until we get to know each other better. And never tell us your salary is negotiable. It's not negotiable. Candidates new to the job market often say that, especially if they are desperate to land a job. You don't ever want to give that answer. You want to answer back with a range because we have to know what you need to live on. If you did your homework, you will know the range.

Suppose the interviewer says to you, "Well, how much are you asking?"

One safe way to respond that establishes that you are a serious candidate, and that you are cutting to the chase: "I'm glad to have your best offer." An even better answer would be: "From my research, and from interviews with other companies, an entry-level position in this market runs into the low forties (or whatever). I would expect the salary range for this job would fall about in there."

That last answer would really impress us. You should know up front what the ranges are, and more importantly, you should know how much you are willing to accept.

Some candidates might respond: "Well, I don't know what salary to ask." Nonsense. If this is not your first job, you obviously know what you earned on your last job. Was that enough for you to live on? If you are looking for a new job, and you already have a job, then a bigger salary is certainly a factor in your search. If you are looking to land your first job, you should still know how much it costs to live in your community of choice. Suppose you decide you need a minimum of $40,000. If the position pays $30,000, you're wasting your time and our time. If you are offered $35,000 and you must have $40,000 to pay your bills, then don't hesitate to let us know that. But also recognize that we may not be prepared to pay more. Never quote a flat salary number to a recruiter. Always give us a range. "I'm looking for between $35,000 and $40,000." And if you happen to be in a job specialty that is in demand, like nuclear engineers or geologists, the range you quote can be wider.

If we posted the salary range, then that's the range. We can't change it for you, even if we wanted to. You can't negotiate the range, so don't try. And don't play games with us and jack up your salary expectations during the interview. Our hiring managers really hate it when you do that, and they hate us even more for letting you waste their time.

Suppose our salary offer doesn't quite meet your needs. Now is the time to factor in some other considerations. Is the job close to your home? Perhaps you live in a big city and our job is right around the corner. That can be worth a lot of money and time you can save by not having to commute. Is this the job of your dreams? Does the company have growth potential? Are the benefits good?

This is a good place to mention that women look at benefits differently than men. If you are a single mom, health insurance, day care (if provided), and flexible hours can be far more important than salary. For some men, work-life balance is an issue. Can you telecommute one or more days a week? Is the company on twelve-hour shifts so you'll only work four days a week? Each of these can be worth having a little less money. If the answer to any of these is "Yes!" then you might want to come in for an interview. Sometimes you will find we have other positions that pay more that you didn't know about. Sometimes we will be so impressed with you that we will create a new opening just for you. (This happened to one of the authors.) Or we may remember you a few months later when another job becomes available.

CHAPTER 11

WHEN IT'S YOUR TURN TO ASK QUESTIONS

Never confuse motion with action.

—Benjamin Franklin

At some point during your interview, the hiring manager will ask if you have any questions. You better have some questions, or she's going to mentally press the button that fires your ejection seat.

Ask questions but don't interrogate us.

It's unnecessary to run through your whole list of questions.

If we like you, and if you like us, there will be plenty of time for questions. Wait until you get our job offer to ask everything. This is when you are the most valuable to us because we are asking you to make a commitment—then you can ask questions to your heart's content.

We said we weren't going to provide an interview Q&A for you. Okay, we lied. There are some basic questions you need to nail down before you can make an informed decision about taking a new job. Here are some questions to consider. Notice how open-ended these are:

- How does this position contribute to company objectives?
- Ask about the management style of the hiring manager. You want to determine if he's into micro-management, empowerment, or somewhere in between.
- How much outside travel is there? (You definitely do NOT want to work for a micro-manager if you travel a lot!) And does this job require me to travel and work on weekends?
- What are the hiring manager's expectations for the position? Which of the listed job responsibilities is the most critical to him and why?
- If you succeed, where will this job take you in five years?
- Is this a new position? (If the position is new, even if it has a job description, you'll have a rare opportunity to structure the work and set all the expectations for the next person who may take your job after you move on to better things. Some people enjoy doing that. Some people hate it.)
- Unless this is a newly created position, what happened to the previous occupant? If she was promoted, that might mean the job is a great stepping stone to advancement. If she is no longer employed here, maybe that's another kind of clue, either about the job itself or about the hiring manager. (Usually we won't tell you if the person was fired or quit or got a better job, but sometimes you can learn by our response because this question might catch us off guard.)
- Ask if you will be working in a team environment. Every company has teams working on various projects, but some firms are actually organized around teaming, with fluid reporting relationships and self-directed work groups. How comfortable are you with ambiguity

and chaos? Some people do their best work free of the corporate leash, even if it means falling off a cliff now and then.

- Some people prefer more direction and clear boundaries. Such people don't do their best work in a team environment—and you know who you are. One clue: Is the office environment an open plan? Are the walls glass or are there no walls at all? Or does everyone have an office with a door? Just because you don't team well doesn't mean you can't work well with others. You're always going to be working with somebody else. And last but not least, make sure you let us know that you are a team player.

One of the things we're going to ask you during your interview is why you picked our firm. Here is what we'd like to hear you say: "I specifically researched your firm and applied because of (this reason) and (this reason) and (this reason)." That response tells us you're a self-starter. We like to hire candidates who make things happen.

Here's what we don't want to hear you say: "I'm here because Gloria called me and set up the interview." Or: "I saw the position on the Internet."

If the company you applied to is publicly held, some recruiters will ask candidates: "What is our stock price?" You had better know the answer. If you weren't interested enough to go to our website or look at the stock quotes in the morning newspaper, what does that tell us about you?

Questions we don't want to hear:

- When do I come to work?
- When do I go to lunch?
- When is quitting time?

And we don't want to hear questions about our benefits plan either. You are here to tell us what you can do for us and not to see what you can get. The time to ask about benefits is when we bring up the subject, or after we make you a job offer. Warning: If you ask us about our day-care facilities, this tells us you have young children. Don't do it. (Not many companies offer this, but it is a huge benefit.) Remember what we said about glass ceilings. If you are a woman, we're going to assume you won't be able to work every day because you have young children. All things being equal, if there are two female candidates for a job, one with children and one that is single, guess who we're going to pick?

CHAPTER 12

THE RESTAURANT INTERVIEW

I am hungry—therefore I am.

—Garfield the Cat

Lunch is often a part of the interview process. Never forget that lunch is not a break in the action; you are still on duty, and you still have to move the ball down the field. Nothing will trip you up faster than embarrassing yourself or your new boss-to-be at the dining table. For any higher-level position where there is expense-account schmoozing to be done, or for a job where you will be living in the public eye or dealing with people important to the firm—customers, investors, elected officials—your behavior in an upscale restaurant is a critical part of your interview. How you handle yourself—how you treat the waitstaff and how you manage your silverware—will be closely observed and reported on to the powers-that-be. A business dinner in an upscale restaurant is no different than the office Christmas party—if your company still has one. Bad behavior in either venue never goes unnoticed. So think of your meal as a test, because that's exactly what it is.

If you are driving to the restaurant, don't smoke in the car. Don't ask to sit in the smoking section. Don't smoke at all.

Some companies, especially health-care providers, won't hire you if they suspect you are a tobacco user. Although, of course we will never tell you that.

Since the hiring manager is probably a frequent customer here, ask her for a recommendation. Let her order for you, or follow her lead. Don't order problem foods like spaghetti or anything that requires you to use both hands, like a hamburger or a meatball sandwich. Finger foods are out (but a cookie for dessert is okay). Don't play with your napkin. Don't tuck it into your shirtfront to protect your tie or blouse. Unfold it, put it on your lap, and leave it alone.

You're going to be doing most of the talking, so don't order anything that requires a lot of chewing. Don't order potatoes or any food heavy enough to make you doze off during a mid-afternoon round of interviews. We're going to be very annoyed with you if you fall asleep on us. Salad is probably your best bet at lunch.

Don't act like you're hungry—you can always eat for real later. Don't tell us you require vegetarian or kosher meals (just order accordingly without making a fuss). This is not a good time to show us how high-maintenance you're going to be. If you're lactose intolerant, don't explain why you don't want the cheese dressing—just quietly ask the waiter to hold the cheese.

Silverware should never be a mystery. Work your way in from the outside. If in doubt, watch your hiring manager and do whatever she does—or consult an etiquette book in advance. If a food item requires cutting, cut enough for one bite at a time. Yes, we know this isn't very efficient, especially if you're used to sawing through everything all at once at home. But dining out isn't supposed to be a timed event, like the hundred-yard dash. It's supposed to be a memorable experience.

Never, never order alcohol—even if someone in your party does so. A few companies still have fancy executive restaurants where alcohol is permitted. Other firms permit on-site drinking on certain occasions or during lunch. Some even allow employees to bring coolers to work on Friday. Always decline alcohol. If somebody offers to buy you a beer or Chablis at the end of your "official" interview day, decline with thanks. "I'd love to, but I'm driving" will get you off the hook without causing offense, and also demonstrate what a safety-conscious employee you're going to be.

If you have religious or personal objections to alcohol, this is a bad time to tell us about your moral values. Contrary to what you learned in school, America really does have a very clear class and caste system; but in our hearts most of us still dislike morally superior people and elitist behavior. That is why America still honors the brave frontier pioneer families in their covered wagons—not the snobby Boston merchant prince who bankrolled their expedition.

Finished eating? Your used silverware should now be resting at a northwest to southeast angle on the upper right quarter of your plate, side by side, not stacked. Don't toss your crumpled napkin onto your plate. Fold it and put it back where you found it.

Don't offer to pick up the check. You are here to be schmoozed.

CHAPTER 13

CLOSING THE DEAL

'Maybe' means No and 'No' means No. Only 'Yes' means Yes.
—Gloria Van Devender-Graves

When the interview is over, shake our hand, thank us, and say it was a real pleasure to meet us. Tell us you want the job. Words to use: "Exciting." "Challenging." "I'm very good at that." The HR manager may not be moved by these words, but the hiring manager will certainly notice. But don't oversell yourself to the point where it sounds like you're running for office.

Don't ask us, "When do you think you'll fill the job?"

Yesterday, if it was up to us. But it's not up to HR. It's the hiring manager's decision. It could be tomorrow. It could be next year. A better question to ask is, "What's the next step?" If we have an idea when you'll hear from us, of course we'll tell you.

But if you hear the dreaded reply, "We still haven't finished interviewing," then you didn't get the job. It's a commonly used rejection response, because we don't want to hurt your feelings with a more direct answer. Rejecting people sucks. We're human, too. We don't want to watch your reaction as we crush your hopes. Of course we're going to take the easiest way out.

Thanks a Lot

As soon as you get home, send a thank-you note by e-mail so we receive it the next morning. You would be surprised at how many candidates forget this simple follow-up act. Sending us a love note is your last chance to stand out from the crowd before we vote on your future.

Your note should thank us for spending time with you and tell us how much you enjoyed yourself. Be sure to mention the position you applied for and how your skills and experience make you the perfect person for the job. We don't care what else you say as long as you thank us.

Thank us and thank everybody you met. If you discussed some bit of personal trivia with one of our managers, mention it again so she'll think well of you: "I especially enjoyed chatting with you about artist Frank Frazetta. I've always wanted to own one of his paintings."

You did get everyone's business card so you have their e-mail address, didn't you? Most people love it when you ask for their card. If you forgot to do that, don't call us back and ask for their addresses. Don't ask our receptionist, either. If you really did drop this ball just in front of the goal line, try to at least be a little creative. Forget the e-mail. Call the main reception number and say something like, "I'm trying to contact Jessie Jones. Could you please put me into her voicemail, or give me her Fax number?"

Don't call or e-mail to harass us about our progress in filling the position. We don't have the time. You can call to check the status of your application, if you filled one out. Some companies will tell you to call and check, which means they probably aren't very organized, so you might want to keep that in mind when it's time to decide if you want to work for them.

Don't call to say you're talking to a few other firms, and that you expect offers from them, so you want to know when you'll hear from us.   .

Don't try to pull that old trick on us. If you don't hear from us in two weeks, go on to the next company on your list. You probably didn't get the job.

References

We don't place much emphasis on your personal references. Your friends will lie for you because they're your friends. What are friends for?

Business references rate a little higher, depending on what they're willing to tell us. Obviously, we'd like to know if you were a good employee and if you came to work on time. Legally, however, we are allowed to ask your previous employer only four things about you: 1) your salary, 2) date of hire, 3) date of termination, 4) job title. And that's it.

At some firms, your former boss is not permitted to answer any questions about you. Only HR can do that because you can sue if you can prove somebody at your old company said something negative about you that prevented you from getting an offer.

Then there's your salary. Your former company doesn't have to tell us what they paid you. We have to state a figure and ask them to confirm it, yes or no.

But don't get cocky. We have all sorts of other ways to find out what we need to know about you.

CHAPTER 14

YOU DIDN'T LIE TO US, DID YOU?

Who are you going to believe? Me, or your lying eyes?
—Groucho Marx

Anything out of order on your resume or your employment application is grounds for immediate dismissal if we hire you.

Here's a news flash, sports fans. Every candidate enhances her resume. But how we react to your creative writing depends on what you chose to exaggerate. It's perfectly acceptable to decorate your personal achievements. For example, maybe you forgot to credit the other colleague who helped you with that big project. Or maybe you forgot to mention that the big sale you made was a team effort. Not a problem. But your salary or your education? Bummer. Don't do it. You will get busted.

Although every company verifies educational experience, about 2 percent of candidates will still try to sneak an unearned degree or two past us. If you lie about this, you will not get a warning. You will be fired.

Never fake a professional certification. If you aren't a Certified Public Accountant or a Fire Prevention Engineer, why would you claim to be? Because you know we're going to check out your claim with your professional society.

Don't give yourself a big pay hike, either. Suppose you will be moving from low-cost Abilene, Kansas, to high-cost, high-tax

Boston, Massachusetts, and you know you can't survive in Beantown on your Kansas salary of $37,000. You might decide to inflate your former pay to $45,000 so your new employer will be forced to match it. Some companies don't check salaries. Most do.

If you get caught in a massive lie like this, we will bust you like a water balloon.

On the other hand, suppose you added a thousand dollars to your former salary. We're not saying it's okay to lie. If we can prove you lied, you won't be hired. But this is one of those gray areas where we're making an overall judgment on you as a person. A large company may spend anywhere from $7,000 to $10,000 on each candidate it interviews, starting with the original advertisement right up through two rounds of interviews, not to mention travel and lodging expenses. Maybe it cost $150,000 just to buy an annual license to use one of the Internet job-recruiting sites, plus our salaries. If you are a great catch, we may choose to note an indiscretion and look the other way. But the point is: Why take a chance like that at all? Besides, a good recruiter can usually tell if an applicant is honest.

What about Background Checks?

Large companies have contracts with security firms that are very good at digging into your past life. These firms started getting a lot of business after September 11, 2001, and business has been good ever since. You're going to be checked out more closely than a German shepherd at a cat fancier's convention if you apply for any federal government job; many state government jobs; all corporate management positions; any job in the public utility, petroleum refining, or chemical industry; and any position requiring a commercial driver's license, pilot's license, or any type of security clearance.

Prior to September 11, all we wanted to know was if you have ever been convicted of a crime. We still want to know that. But now we're also very interested to know if you might be a terrorist. Background checks take awhile; so if you pass the initial screening, you'll start your new job while the results continue to roll in.

> If there are any little surprises in your past that could make us nervous, like your nine visits to the Middle East, it might be a good idea to tell us about them when we make you the offer.

An indiscretion like writing a couple of bad checks or skimping on child support payments won't bother us much if you come clean ahead of time and can prove you've made restitution. But not everyone loves a reformed sinner. A financial institution will come down on you a lot harder for floating checks than the auto industry. It's a judgment call on your part.

Some positions require passing a pre-employment physical exam. If, for example, your new job involves driving thousands of miles a year, and we discover you forgot to tell us you're legally blind in one eye, we're going to withdraw our offer. You can sue us, but you won't win because we can prove you lied to us. Then there's the drug screen. Naturally, you told the doctor in advance about any prescription medicines you might be using.

However, if the drug screen shows you've been sampling chemicals not normally found at the corner pharmacy, or if we discover excessive traces of alcohol in you, guess what? You won't be coming to work here. A word to the wise: Don't have that poppy-seed bun for breakfast. Poppy seed is one of those gifts that keep on giving. It may show up as a positive for heroin in the drug screen long after you've forgotten how tasty it was.

CHAPTER 15

POSTMORTEM

I feel very humble, but I think I have the strength of character to fight it.

—Bob Hope

You're probably going to find this topic a bit depressing, but it's a critical part of the hiring process. Besides, we promised you an inside look (sort of like going behind the scenes and into the kitchen of your favorite restaurant). Certainly after the information we're about to provide, you'll never view interviews the same way again!

By now, the HR recruiter has finished with you. His only remaining role concerning you will be to communicate the good or the not-so-good news about your future as decided by the hiring manager.

Although the hiring manager has the final say about you, he will usually do the courtesy of asking his direct reports (subordinates) and peers for an opinion, especially if you'll be interacting with them. (Exception: If the hiring manager has a very strong personality, his direct reports will realize their role in this process is only a formality. In other words, everybody but the job candidate already knows an offer is forthcoming. Unfortunately, strong managers, especially if they are very good at their jobs, make a lot of enemies. They don't hang around very long. They are usually kicked upstairs because they know too much to let a competitor get their hands on them. Or if they are especially annoying by being right more often than the chief executive, they will be fired. But working for one of them can teach you a lot before either of those things happens).

Every company has its own method for comparing notes about job candidates.

In a few well-regulated companies, the HR recruiter may take the lead in asking each manager how they feel about you. More likely, the hiring manager will just drop by everybody's office to gather impressions. More often still, there's a postmortem— a sort of round-robin conference where everybody shares an opinion about you. It's an informal process, but as far as you're concerned, it's as final as the last flight from Saigon.

Let's suppose, for the sake of this example, that you and several other candidates were interviewed over the course of a day. This is actually pretty typical, since interviews have to be scheduled when all the relevant managers are in the office at the same time. Because they are attending to the firm's business between interviews with you and the other candidates, it can be pretty hard for managers to remember a lot of specifics about each of you, especially if the postmortem is delayed for a day or two.

Sad fact: Nobody wants to make the mistake of supporting a candidate who might not work out, so nobody is going to walk the plank for you.

The first manager to start the postmortem may even mention something negative about you until she sees how the wind is blowing.

Others may pile on at that point, or they may play it down the middle and say something both positive and negative. Or they may say nothing at all. Negative comments will most often be directed at your mannerisms, not your qualifications, because that may be the only thing they can remember without sneaking another quick look at your resume, which they have probably misplaced. And if some managers speak positively about you, the naysayers and the uncommitted know they can always jump back on board. If every comment is negative, you won't be offered the job, but at least nobody will get blamed for making a bad hire.

Yes, we know. It's totally unfair. But didn't we say the interview process is subjective?

You'll notice in this example the hiring manager never voices an opinion. Like the chief justice of the U.S. Supreme Court, he always votes last so as not to influence the other jurists. You'll also see each of the above-mentioned behaviors. Note that the direction of this postmortem is completely reversed by the low-ranking office supervisor, who in this particular case, was invited to participate more as a courtesy than in the hope she might actually contribute anything useful. Also note that the office supervisor ferreted out a particularly telling piece of critical information that all five managers missed. A chance event, you might say, except that life is full of unexpected happenings.

> **HIRING MANAGER:** What is your impression of Molly Leigh?
>
> **FIRST LINE MANAGER:** She never made eye contact with me.
>
> **SECOND LINE MANAGER:** She didn't know what to do with her hands. She must have had sixteen bracelets on each wrist. I couldn't hear myself think with all that clanking.
>
> **THIRD LINE MANAGER:** (*Shakes head slightly. Maybe he agrees with the preceding comment. Maybe not.*)

FOURTH LINE MANAGER: I liked her. But she wasn't very animated.

OFFICE SUPERVISOR: That's because she was nervous. You kept her waiting for ages. I had a nice chat with her. Did you know she has fourteen direct reports? And four of them are in salary bands higher than hers? No wonder she wants to leave that crummy job.

FIRST MANAGER: Fourteen. That's a lot.

SECOND MANAGER: She's certainly very qualified.

THIRD MANAGER: (*Casually consults resume.*) She's been in that job for eight years. A guy in my bridge club works for that company. If she lasted that long, she must be good. She would probably enjoy working for us a lot more.

FOURTH MANAGER: I like the fact that she's going to night school to study computer science. That might be useful when we upgrade the robotics software next year.

HIRING MANAGER: That's it, then. I'll call HR and ask them to make Molly an offer.

CHAPTER 16

OKAY, YOU GOT THE OFFER! WHAT ABOUT NEGOTIATIONS?

You see things; and you say 'Why?' But I dream things that never were; and I say 'Why not?'

—George Bernard Shaw

There is a lot less to this topic than you might imagine, so it won't take long. Let's start with your salary. As we've already stated, you can negotiate to a point, but the salary range itself is never negotiable. If the job pays less than you need to live on, it's time to saddle up and ride on, because there's nothing we can do for you. The job offer will mention your starting salary. Any attempt on your part to negotiate a higher figure will make everyone at our company sore at you before you start.

Benefits? They are what they are. If we don't have what you expected, go away. We can't make an exception for you.

Extra vacation time? Not hardly. Everybody gets the same deal. A seasoned employee who is a valuable addition to the firm might be able to engineer an unofficial agreement with his supervisor for more time off—but that's what it is, unofficial. If your supervisor gets promoted, don't expect his replacement to honor your bargain.

Expense accounts, laptop computers, cell phones and pagers, personal digital assistants, digital cameras, and company cars are not perks or entitlements—they're business tools. If your job calls for the use of one or all of these tools, you'll have them. They are not subject to negotiation.

If there is a waiting period to take advantage of the company match to the 401(k), sorry, then there's a waiting period. If we don't have what you want, why do you want to work here?

Some things you can negotiate:

- **Your starting date.** In return for an early starting date, ask if the firm will throw in an extra plane ticket back home to visit your family if you can't move right away.
- **Your first unofficial performance review with your supervisor.** Corporations have annual reviews, but your boss should be willing to have a serious discussion with you about your performance after ninety days on the job.
- **Company assistance with any outside educational or training courses to make you a more valuable employee.** Nail this down early because in some firms, educational expenses are a departmental not a corporate expense. If it's not in your group budget, you aren't going.
- **Moving expenses.** These are as fixed as the orbit of Mars, depending on your salary band, and often non-negotiable. But the company may be willing to make an exception for certain items normally not covered such as your boat or horse or lawn gear, such as a jungle gym or playhouse (disassembled).
- **Penalty payments.** If you're renting back home, the company might be willing to pay the penalty for breaking your lease.
- **Family time off.** If a critical family event requires your presence in the next few months (graduations, christenings, weddings) before you have sufficient time to accrue enough vacation with your new company, now is a good time to make your wishes known.

The Signing Bonus

Many companies have a discretionary fund called a signing bonus to throw at a new hire. A signing bonus may be intended to compensate you for moving from low-cost Alabama to high-cost Connecticut. The signing bonus may be intended to cover the cost of whatever moving expenses we didn't pick up for you. The signing bonus may be our gift to you for any discrepancies between our benefits plan and the plan you gave up to join us.

Or it might be to lure you to frigid, gloomy Minnesota when you'd much rather work for our competitor in sunny San Diego. Or maybe we just like you a lot, and we want you to feel good about coming to work for us.

If You Turn Down Our Offer, Is Our Door Still Open to You?

What planet are you from?

Why did you waste our time? Our managers have just gone through a lengthy interview process, the negotiations and paperwork, and an expensive background check. The hiring manager's supervisor—and sometimes even the president of the firm—has personally approved the decision to extend an offer to you, and now you tell us you don't want the job. If you turn down our job offer, our door will *never* be open to you again. You're not ever coming back here, and believe us when we say we'll make sure you don't get in.

CHAPTER 17

AFTER THE FAT LADY SINGS

You have your way. I have my way. As for the right way, the correct way and the only way, it does not exist.

—Friedrich Nietzsche

You can interview well, and someone may not like your qualifications or your personality enough to offer you the job you want, even if you appear to have the right skills and experience. There's no accounting for personal chemistry. Life is unfair and the competition is fierce. In today's job market, there are so many unemployed and underemployed candidates looking for work that a hiring manager can literally afford to wait for the perfect person. So it goes. March on! Victory may be as close as your next interview.

Some words to the wise: Be professional. Be honest. Be yourself.

Do your best. After each new experience, hold your own little postmortem. Ask yourself: What can I learn from this?

Sure, rejections hurt. But don't be discouraged. Out of the hundreds of resumes we read and threw away, there was something special about yours that made us pick up the phone and dial your number.

That's worth keeping in mind.

CHAPTER 18

ARE YOU A GAZELLE OR A LION?

No pain, no palm; no thorns, no throne; no gall, no glory; no cross, no crown.

— William Penn

Each morning in Africa the gazelles awaken, knowing they must outrun the fastest lion if they want to stay alive.

Each morning in Africa the lions awaken, knowing they must run faster than the slowest gazelle, or they will starve to death.

The meaning of this tale?

It makes no difference whether you are a gazelle or a lion. When the sun rises, you had better be running!